The wall of remembrance at the USS *Arizona* Memorial will be among the locations for commemorative events which will mark the 75th anniversary of the Pearl Harbor attack. *Courtesy, PA*

PEARL HARBOR:
THE 75TH ANNIVERSARY

On December 7, 2016, America and the world will mark the 75th anniversary of the attack on Pearl Harbor with a series of commemorative events focused on those taking place in Hawaii.

In the time since the attack, the date has been honoured with various memorials and commemorations to pay tribute to those who were killed that Sunday, and more generally to the millions who lost their lives during the course of the Pacific War.

In the months after the Japanese offensive, 'Remember December 7' and 'Remember Pearl Harbor' became slogans used to incite hatred of the enemy and unite Americans behind the common cause of forcing unconditional Japanese defeat.

The words have stayed the same, but the sentiment has softened in the years since to a point where all those who perished and suffered as a result of that infamous Sunday are remembered.

Among those gathered on Oahu to pay their respects each year are those who witnessed it for themselves, coming together to honour fallen friends and colleagues; they being the only ones who can truly understand the horrors to which they were subjected.

Even as their numbers become fewer with each passing year, we must never forget these brave souls and the thousands more who never got the chance to share their harrowing story.

> **"Throughout the entire action, and through all the arduous labours which followed, there was never the slightest sign of faltering or of cowardice. The actions of the officers and men were all wholly commendable; their spirit was marvellous; there was no panic, no shirking nor flinching, and words fail in attempting to describe the truly magnificent display of courage, discipline, and devotion to duty of all officers and men."**
>
> *Pearl Harbor survivor*

which would eventually claim the lives of more than 20 million of its inhabitants.

My interest in Pearl Harbor is historical, and that's what I wanted this volume to be about, but remaining detached enough to present the cold hard facts has been a challenge – although it's one I feel privileged to have been able to take on.

In my own small way, I've been able to remember the sacrifices that were made, the hardships which were endured and the incredible bravery and determination that ordinary people, no different to myself, were able to summon in the face of adversity.

I certainly hope my admiration and respect for all those who were involved on that 'day of infamy' and the wider conflicts of which it was a part are reflected in this volume, and that my efforts to present a fair and balanced narrative of what was occurring on both sides of the Pacific comes across.

In my own humble opinion, the Pearl Harbor attack is the single-most defining episode of the last century, and we're still trying to fully understand and learn the effects of it today. To say that I'd like you to 'enjoy' this read would seem strange given the topic, but I hope you find my presentation of Pearl Harbor history to be an interesting and informative one.

Jack Harrison
Author

Acknowledgements

I owe a great deal of thanks to a great many people and organisations for helping make this publication a reality. Professionally I must first praise the wealth of Pearl Harbor related resources which exist, allowing this fascinating and historically important tale to be told. More specifically to this volume, mentions must go to production editor Dan Sharp, designer Craig Lamb, cover artist Ronnie Olsthoorn, cover designer Justin Blackamore and picture desk operators Paul Fincham and Jonathan Schofield who have used their collective expertise to hone my words and then bring them to life in the pages you see before you. On a final personal note I would like to express my appreciation for the support and understanding of friends, family and loved ones throughout the time it has taken to compile *Pearl Harbor: The 75th Anniversary*. It has required a great deal of time, effort and concentration – not to mention a few late nights – to reach this final product and I would not have been able to achieve it without their help.

CONTENTS

A US military photographer surveys the devastation caused by the Japanese attack on Pearl Harbor as smoke rises into the skies above Battleship Row. *Courtesy, PA*

AUTHOR: Jack Harrison
jharrison@mortons.co.uk
PAGE DESIGN: Craig Lamb
design_lamb@btinternet.com
COVER DESIGN: Justin Blackamore
COVER ARTWORK: Ronnie Olsthoorn
aviationart.aero
PRODUCTION EDITOR: Dan Sharp
REPROGRAPHICS: Paul Fincham
REPROGRAPHICS: Jonathan Schofield
ADVERTISING: Sue Keily
skeily@mortons.co.uk
TRADE SALES: John Sharratt
tradesales@mortons.co.uk
MARKETING MANAGER: Charlotte Park
COMMERCIAL DIRECTOR: Nigel Hole
PUBLISHING DIRECTOR: Dan Savage
PUBLISHER: Steve O'Hara

PRINTED BY:
William Gibbons and Sons, Wolverhampton

ISBN: 978-1-911276-05-0

PUBLISHED BY:
Mortons Media Group Ltd,
Media Centre, Morton Way
Horncastle, Lincolnshire LN9 6JR
Tel: 01507 529529

PEARL HARBOR: THE 75TH ANNIVERSARY

Honolulu Star-Bulletin 1st EXTRA

Evening Bulletin, Est. 1882, Vol. L, No. 1379
Hawaiian Star, Vol. XLVIII, No. 15274

8 PAGES—HONOLULU TERRITORY OF HAWAII, U. S. A., SUNDAY, DECEMBER 7, 1941—8 PAGES ★ PRICE FIVE CENTS

WAR!

OAHU BOMBED BY JAPANESE PLANES

(Associated Press by Transpacific Telephone)

SAN FRANCISCO, Dec. 7.—President Roosevelt announced this morning that Japanese planes had attacked Manila and Pearl Harbor.

SIX KNOWN DEAD, 21 INJURED, AT EMERGENCY HOSPITAL

Attack Made On Island's Defense Areas

WASHINGTON, Dec. 7.—Text of a White House announcement detailing the attack on the Hawaiian islands is:

"The Japanese attacked Pearl Harbor from the air and all naval and military activities on the island of Oahu, principal American base in the Hawaiian islands."

Oahu was attacked at 7:55 this morning by Japanese planes.

The Rising Sun, emblem of Japan, was seen on plane wing tips.

Wave after wave of bombers streamed through the clouded morning sky from the southwest and flung their missiles on a city resting in peaceful Sabbath calm.

According to an unconfirmed report received at the governor's office, the Japanese force that attacked Oahu reached island waters aboard two small airplane carriers.

It was also reported that at the governor's office either an attempt had been made to bomb the USS Lexington, or that it had been bombed.

CITY IN UPROAR

Within 10 minutes the city was in an uproar. As bombs fell in many parts of the city, and in defense areas the defenders of the islands went into quick action.

Army intelligence officers at Ft. Shafter announced officially shortly after 9 a. m. the fact of the bombardment by an enemy but long previous army and navy had taken immediate measures in defense.

"Oahu is under a sporadic air raid," the announcement said.

"Civilians are ordered to stay off the streets until further notice."

CIVILIANS ORDERED OFF STREETS

The army has ordered that all civilians stay off the streets and highways and not use telephones.

Evidence that the Japanese attack has registered some hits was shown by three billowing pillars of smoke in the Pearl Harbor and Hickam field area.

All navy personnel and civilian defense workers, with the exception of women, have been ordered to duty at Pearl Harbor.

The Pearl Harbor highway was immediately a mass of racing cars.

A trickling stream of injured people began pouring into the city emergency hospital a few minutes after the bombardment started.

Thousands of telephone calls almost swamped the Mutual Telephone Co. which put extra operators on duty.

At The Star-Bulletin office the phone calls deluged the single operator and it was impossible for this newspaper, for sometime, to handle the flood of calls. Here also an emergency operator was called.

HOUR OF ATTACK—7:55 A. M.

An official army report from department headquarters, made public shortly before 11 is that the first attack was at 7:55 a. m.

Witnesses said they saw at least 50 airplanes in the Pearl Harbor.

The attack centered in the Pearl Harbor, Army authorities said:

"The rising sun was seen on the wing tips of the airplanes.

Although martial law had not been declared officially, the city of Honolulu was operating under M-Day conditions.

It is reliably reported that enemy objectives under attack were Wheeler field, Hickam field, Kaneohe bay and naval air station and Pearl Harbor.

Some enemy planes were reported shot down.

The body of the pilot was seen in a plane burning at Wahiawa.

Oahu appeared to be taking calmly after the first uproar of queries.

ANTIAIRCRAFT GUNS IN ACTION

First indication of the raid came shortly before 8 this morning when antiaircraft guns around Pearl Habor began sending up a thunderous barrage.

At the same time a vast cloud of black smoke arose from the naval base and also from Hickam field where flames could be seen.

BOMB NEAR GOVERNOR'S MANSION

Shortly before 9:30 a bomb fell near Washington Place, the residence of the governor. Governor Poindexter and Secretary Charles M. Hite were there.

It was reported that the bomb killed an unidentified Chinese man across the street in front of the Schuman Carriage Co. where windows were broken.

C. E. Daniels, a welder, found a fragment of shell or bomb at South and Queen Sts. which he brought into the City Hall. This fragment weighed about a pound.

At 10:05 a. m. today Governor Poindexter telephoned to The Star-Bulletin announcing he has declared a state of emergency for the entire territory.

He announced that Edouard L. Doty, executive secretary of the major disaster council, has been appointed director under the M-Day law's provisions.

Governor Poindexter urged all residents of Honolulu to remain off the street, and the people of the territory to remain calm.

Mr. Doty reported that all major disaster council wardens and medical units were on duty within a half hour of the time the alarm was given.

Workers employed at Pearl Harbor were ordered at 10:10 a. m. not to report at Pearl Harbor.

The mayor's major disaster council was to meet at the city hall at about 10:30 this morning.

At least two Japanese planes were reported at Hawaiian department headquarters to have been shot down.

One of the planes was shot down at Ft. Kamehameha and the other back of the Wa—

Turn to Page 8, Column 1

Hundreds See City Bombed

Hundreds of Honolulans who hurried to the top of Punchbowl soon after bombs began to fall, saw spread out before them the whole panorama of surprise attack and defense.

Far off over Pearl Harbor the white sky was polka-dotted with anti-aircraft smoke.

Rolling away from the navy base were billowing clouds of ugly black smoke. Sometimes a burst of flames reddened the black sources of the smoke.

Nearer, from the silver-surfaced mouth of the harbor a flotilla of destroyers streamed to battle, smoke pouring from their stacks.

Turn to Page 8, Column 1

Names of Dead and Injured

The city emergency hospital reported at 10:30 a list of 6 killed and 21 injured.

The complete list will be carried later. Here is a partial list:

Peter Lopes, 24, of 3641 Kaimuki Rd. St, was reported at 9:30 a. m. to be in serious condition from wounds in the upper abdomen.

Bernice Gonzales, 12, 2745 Kalihi St, is suffering from a mangled thigh, lacerations on the right leg and left arm.

A Portuguese girl, unidentified, 10 years old, died on arrival from puncture wounds.

Another victim who died on arrival was Frank Ohashi, 30, 2708 Kamanaiki St, from puncture wounds in the chest.

Cornelia Broadby, 36, Moanalua gardens, was released from the hospital after treatment for lacerations.

Three were reported injured and one reported killed from the bomb that fell at Fort and School Sts.

Schools Closed

All schools on Oahu, both public and private will remain closed until further notice, Edouard L. Doty, territorial director of civilian defense announced at 11 a. m. today. This does not apply elsewhere in the territory.

Editorial

HAWAII MEETS THE CRISIS

Honolulu and Hawaii will meet the emergency of war today as Honolulu and Hawaii have met emergencies in the past—coolly, calmly and with immediate and complete support of the officials, officers and troops who are in charge.

Governor Poindexter and the army and navy leaders have called upon the public to remain calm; for civilians who have no essential business on the streets to stay off, and for every man and woman to do his duty.

That request, coupled with the measures promptly taken to meet the situation that has suddenly and terribly developed, will be needed.

Hawaii will do its part—as a loyal American territory. In this crisis, every difference of race, creed and color will be submerged in the one desire and determination to play the part that Americans always play in crisis.

BULLETIN

Additional Star-Bulletin extras today will cover the latest developments in this war move.

Courtesy, PA

INTRODUCTION

As the first of 353 Japanese aircraft broke through the clouds just a few miles off the coast of Oahu on the morning of December 7, 1941, it brought to an end America's long-held policy of remaining officially neutral in the devastating war which was engulfing the world.

By the end of the offensive which ensued, the US had lost more than 2000 military personnel in a sneak attack, Japan was revelling in what it believed to be a great and decisive tactical victory – and neither could yet imagine the way in which the events of that fateful Sunday had already changed the world.

For America, torn between nearly 165 years of isolationism and a growing desire for a global role, the attack on Pearl Harbor sent a unifying wave across the nation which now entered the conflict with an overwhelming vigour and sense of resolve. Westwards, across the Pacific, Japan followed its success in Hawaii with a dominant military campaign in South East Asia where it gained a significant early upper hand.

Soon, however, the US would begin a slow but decisive fight back which would result in several key victories, and culminate in the unleashing of the world's first atomic weapons in Hiroshima and Nagasaki.

It's through this historical context that I have attempted to tell the fascinating and often harrowing story of Pearl Harbor – not just what happened that day, but the complex set of circumstances which are inexorably linked to why it occurred, how it unfolded and the significant impact felt by both the belligerents involved and the wider world.

Courtesy, PA

CHAPTER 1

ISOLATIONISM

American foreign policy before 1941

Today the world is accustomed to America being a far-reaching global superpower. Before the attack on Pearl Harbor however, and particularly before the First World War, the country's political and military leaders had stood firmly behind a policy of isolationism…

THIS LEAGUE OF NATIONS BRIDGE WAS DESIGNED BY THE PRESIDENT OF THE U·S·A·

THE GAP IN

Against the backdrop of Franklin D Roosevelt's memorable speech to a joint session of Congress, the United States formally declared war on the Japanese Empire on December 8, 1941 – a direct response to the attack on Pearl Harbor.

Not yet 200 years old as a nation, America was now embroiled in the Second World War. It was no stranger to this kind of mass conflict however; in its relatively short history the US had endured the War of Independence, a civil war, involvement in the First World War and several confrontations with European and South American forces as it expanded and established its territory to the west coast and beyond throughout the 19th century.

Despite this familiarity with military engagements, it wasn't until the attack on Pearl Harbor that the US embarked on a permanent outward-looking role in foreign affairs, instead of focusing its gaze on what was happening within its own borders, or just outside of them. The American tendency towards isolationism came, partly by design and partly by default, from the core ideals on which the nation was founded.

America's pursuit of isolationism was never more evident than in 1919 when the Senate voted against joining the League of Nations which President Woodrow Wilson had helped to develop in the aftermath of the First World War. This cartoon – The Gap in the Bridge – appeared in *Punch* magazine on December 10 of that year and depicts the United States as the missing keystone of the League of Nations arch. Uncle Sam smoking a cigar symbolises American wealth. ☺

THE BRIDGE.

America declares its intentions

So monumental was the notion that a small band of revolutionaries could forge a new nation from a disparate collection of colonial territories, that turning the dream of America into a reality was the sole purpose of its founding fathers. The way in which the fledgling country would interact with the wider world was far from their immediate thoughts, but because the set of ideals and values they laid out in the Declaration of Independence of 1776 became so fundamental to every facet of the American existence, the desire for freedom soon became a strong tendency towards isolationism in its foreign policy.

It's not hard to see how this concept developed. The declaration enshrines the right to 'life, liberty and the pursuit of happiness,' free from foreign interference or oppression, so it stands to reason that a country founded on that basic idea should not seek to extend its influence beyond its own peoples.

A far more compelling and practical reason why a role in foreign affairs wasn't pursued in America's infancy was that it simply didn't have sufficient power or resources. And what measure it did have of each was devoted to its domestic goals, and then to ensuring its own survival once freedom had been achieved. This idea, that all efforts should be focused on advancement at home rather than interference abroad, would become so entrenched that nothing short of a direct assault on the American way of life could shake it.

This map depicting America in 1750, with modern day borders added for perspective, demonstrates the incredible challenge faced by the original 13 US colonies – the red British-owned territory – to establish a new nation. With a mass of French-owned land to the west, the Model Treaty and the Treaty of Alliance were both vital. *Courtesy, Pinpin* ✱

While America had neither the desire nor the realistic capability of being a player on a global scale at that time, its fortunes were nevertheless tied to those of its European contemporaries; in fact, its entire future depended on their actions.

By the time the Second Continental Congress had formed in 1775, the Revolutionary War was already under way and it was clear to the delegates of the colonies that they would require political, economic and possibly military support from France.

As the de facto national government, the Continental Congress began negotiating with foreign nations on behalf of the colonies and dispatched delegate Silas Deane to France in 1776 to secure support for its independence campaign, the same year in which highly respected American diplomat Benjamin Franklin became the US ambassador to the country.

The Declaration of Independence set out the rights that the 13 American colonies believed to be 'self-evident' and the content of the document quickly spread throughout the land. Pictured is John Nixon, reading the words aloud from the steps of Independence Hall in Philadelphia, July 8, 1776. ⊙

READING THE DECLARATION OF INDEPENDENCE BY JOHN NIXON, FROM THE STEPS OF INDEPENDENCE HALL, PHILADELPHIA, JULY 8, 1776.—DRAWN BY E. A. ABBEY.—[SEE ARTICLE "'76," PAGE 574.]

America's early foreign policy

Later in the year, the Continental Congress would approve the Model Treaty with France, a document drafted by Massachusetts delegate and future president John Adams, which would become a template for subsequent international agreements. What makes it so significant is that its primary focus was not to shape or dictate the course of general foreign affairs, but to ensure that the greatest possible number of commercial opportunities were available to the young nation, which had already spent vast sums of colonial cash in its fight against the British Empire.

The opportunity to prosper and make full use of its sought-after national resources was of paramount importance for the US and it began to lay that foundation by ensuring the Model Treaty had within its terms that America would accept no military personnel from France or submit to any French authority as part of any alliance. It was simply about the Continental Congress, and the governing bodies which would follow it, having the chance to present terms of trade.

It wasn't until 1778 that France and America reached an agreement, and when they did it was not the Model Treaty but the Treaty of Alliance which was formally adopted. There were only slight differences to Adams' original, but importantly these covered both nations not seeking territorial gains in areas that each had a claim on – the US in North America and France in the Caribbean. It also included a statement that the American colonies had no designs on Spanish territories.

With a formal alliance with France and support from Spain, the Revolutionary War turned in America's favour as the 1770s came to a conclusion, and by the end of the decade and the beginning of the next, the Continental Congress was preparing peace terms which would see the British Empire recognise America as an independent nation.

Foreign policy had been vital to the

One of America's founding fathers, Benjamin Franklin enjoyed an almost celebrity status in France during his time as ambassador and was influential in securing French backing for US independence. This carbonic alloy engraving was drawn by French artist Charles-Nicolas Cochin during Franklin's time in the country. ○

imminent American victory, but although assistance had come from abroad its alliances were not the sort of complex agreements which would leave it vulnerable to either France or Spain asserting their own authority within the proposed American borders.

On September 3, 1783, the Treaty of Paris was signed by Great Britain and the United States of America to officially bring the Revolutionary War to an end.

In 1789 the first US Congress would create the Department of Foreign Affairs, but this would soon be renamed the Department of State, as we know it today, and the symbolic change further demonstrated that America's overseas concerns were about ensuring its own prosperity and not meddling in the business of others.

The new government's commitment to this approach would be sternly tested in 1792 as Britain and France went to war and the French looked to the United States for backing, invoking the terms of the Treaty of Alliance. With his cabinet unanimously behind him, President George Washington declared neutrality and announced that the 1778 agreement no longer applied; the first of three key events which would set a precedent for the American isolationism that would remain largely intact until 1941.

A fragile status quo had existed between the US and Great Britain in the decade since the end of the Revolutionary War, but the latter's conflict with France – or more importantly how America would react to it – saw tensions flare once again. The second event that helped shape US foreign policy for the years to come was the signing of the Treaty of Amity, Commerce and Navigation, Between His Britannic Majesty and the United States of America; better known as the Jay Treaty.

After the US had gained its independence, Britain had become its most fruitful trading partner and neither country wanted to slip back into a costly and ruinous state of war. In order to avoid this, the Jay Treaty settled some of the questions concerning boundaries and trade that had lingered since the Treaty of Paris and, despite opposition from prominent members of the American government who still harboured strong anti-British sentiment, it was signed and is credited with averting an all-out war between the two nations, something America felt it simply could not afford at the time. By choosing the best course for American trade and commerce over international friendships or rivalries, Washington also set a foreign policy example which his predecessors had to follow. With the president's actions having set out the stall for American isolationism, his words during his farewell address of 1796 cemented the policy in place.

He declared: "The great rule of conduct for us in regard to foreign nations is in extending our commercial relations, to have with them as little political connection as possible. So far as we have already formed engagements, let them be fulfilled with

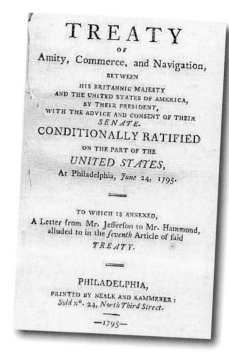

A 1795 pamphlet containing the text of the Jay Treaty, published in Pennsylvania. ○

perfect good faith. Here let us stop. Europe has a set of primary interests which to us have none; or a very remote relation."

By this time, Washington was a revered figure across America. He was the war hero who led 13 separate colonies to a victory against one of the largest and most powerful empires the world had ever seen, he was the political leader whose shrewd guidance had allowed a nation to establish itself and then he established his legacy by stepping down as president after eight years because he didn't believe in one person holding power for longer. His words were as close to gospel as a non-religious figure could be, and they consecrated America's isolationist stance as steadfast national policy.

America's first president set his country on the course of isolationism. This painting of George Washington hangs in the National Portrait Gallery at the Smithsonian Institution, Washington, DC. ○

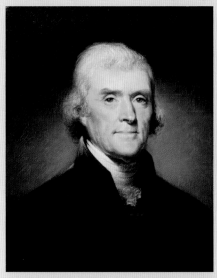

KEY PLAYERS: Presidents Thomas Jefferson (left) and James Madison (right) played important roles in the direction of US foreign policy in the 19th century, continuing on the path set by Washington. ✪

A newspaper cartoon published in 1912 uses the iconic image of Uncle Sam to explain the Monroe Doctrine, showing the American continent in the Western Hemisphere separated from the rest of the world. ✪

The Monroe Doctrine and Manifest Destiny

Thomas Jefferson, America's third president and the man considered to have had most influence on the Declaration of Independence, continued to develop Washington's ideas during his time in office, stating in his own inaugural address in 1801 that the US should maintain 'peace, commerce, and honest friendship with all nations, entangling alliances with none'.

Just 11 years later however, during the presidency of James Madison, America would once again find itself coming up against the British in the War of 1812. As has been the case with many, if not all, American military engagements in its entire history, the root cause was a threat to US trade.

While the three year conflict was costly, America was able to repulse British invasions of many key territories and retain its independence. The eventual outcome sparked a wave of nationalist sentiment too.

If the decisive actions and resounding words of political leaders had set out America's foreign policy before then a perceived second victory against Great Britain sealed it once and for all; the US would not involve itself in foreign affairs unless it faced a direct threat or assault to its future.

As America developed, so did the world around it, particularly Latin America where many countries were facing their own battles to break the chains of European imperial rule. In response, President James Monroe delivered a speech to Congress in 1823 and its content would become a long-standing template for how US leaders approached world affairs.

The Monroe Doctrine, as it came to be known, put forward three main concepts: separate spheres of influence for the Americas and Europe, non-colonisation and non-interventionism. The aim was to

prevent the European powers from retaining dominion over Latin or South American states which wanted independence, or those which had already established self-rule, and while there was a publicised and probably genuine desire to see the American ideal of democracy spread across the continent, the driving force behind it was protecting US access to the new and emerging markets south of its borders.

Across the Atlantic, Britain showed some support for the move as it had a desire to see the demise of Spanish colonialism. In the months before the Monroe Doctrine, British Foreign Minister George Canning had suggested a joint statement which compelled other European powers to refrain from intervening in Central and South America but Secretary of State John Quincy Adams rejected this out of hand believing it to be tantamount to the kind of entangling alliance which Jefferson had warned against. Instead, Monroe's address became a unilateral declaration that 'the American continents... are henceforth not to be considered as subjects for future colonisation by European powers'.

In return, the US pledged to avoid political involvement in the affairs of Europe, Monroe explicitly stating: "In the wars of the European powers, in matters relating to themselves, we have never taken part, nor does it comport with our policy to do so. It is only when our rights are invaded, or seriously menaced that we resent injuries, or make preparations for our defence." With the doctrine becoming such a cornerstone of American foreign policy, it was a promise that future presidents and governments would strive to keep, and only the most catastrophic of circumstances would force a change.

Less than 50 years after it resolutely declared its independence, America was now truly free as the European

President James Monroe (left) who delivered the Monroe Doctrine and Secretary of State John Quincy Adams (right) who was its architect. ✪

President Theodore Roosevelt expanded US interests overseas, but it was confined to the Western Hemisphere which was an accepted policy under the Monroe Doctrine. ✪

Titled *American Progress*, this 1872 painting by John Gast represents Manifest Destiny. The idealised scene shows Americans moving westwards protected by Columbia – representing America and dressed in a Roman toga to signify republicanism – bringing with her modern technology in the form of railways and telegraph lines. ✪

powers adhered to the Monroe Doctrine and allowed the US to push south and westwards, edging its frontier ever closer to the Pacific coastline. In 1845 an article was published on the annexation of Texas in which author John L O'Sullivan first employed the term Manifest Destiny which would become a phrase synonymous with American attitudes towards its rapid expansion: the US not only *could* stretch across the continent, but it was destined to finish the job of the early settlers and conquer the new world.

As with many chapters in American history the story has been idealised, and in among glorious tales of the race to the west exist the harsh realities of Native American removal, slavery and the brutal treatment of various peoples who already occupied the land. From 1861 to 1865 the US also endured its own civil war and although the nation was reunited by President Abraham Lincoln it left a bitter divide and resulted in the deaths of more than half a million American soldiers and civilians.

In terms of foreign affairs, however, not a lot changed during this time. The European nations which had once laid claim to vast swathes of the American continent could not take advantage of any vulnerability the US may have suffered during its period of infighting and as it went through its period of reconstruction, Manifest Destiny continued in earnest and by 1890 San Francisco had become America's eighth most populous city.

Once US expansion had reached the west coast there was a natural inclination to look further, however it would take the sort of 'extraordinary emergency' that Washington had described to draw America across its borders.

When the USS *Maine* exploded and sank in Havana harbour, Cuba, in 1898, killing 266 men, it was the Spanish who were

blamed and a four-month-long Spanish-American War resulted in America taking control of Spain's worldwide empire which included Cuba, Puerto Rico, the Philippines and Guam. In the same year as the conflict, Hawaii had voluntarily become an American territory with full US citizenship for its residents; although it was American-born or descended islanders who secured the effective overthrow of the monarchy and not native Hawaiians.

In the early 1900s, the administration of President Theodore Roosevelt continued to intervene in Latin and South American affairs but, because this was done under the auspices of the Monroe Doctrine and Manifest Destiny, the wider American government was at ease with these developments. Trouble was brewing in Europe however as rival nations built towards the First World War and soon enough the US would face the prospect of being dragged back in to conflicts in the European sphere.

The annexation of Hawaii announced in the *Pacific Commercial Advertiser*, July 14, 1898. ✪

The USS *Maine* entering Havana harbour in January 1898. It would explode in the port just three weeks later, sparking a war between America and Spain. ✪

LEFT: America's 28th President Woodrow Wilson has not achieved the same revered status in history as the likes of Washington or Jefferson, or the later John F Kennedy and Ronald Reagan. Of all the holders of the office, however, his influence on foreign policy has perhaps been the greatest and it's his actions that paved the way for an isolationist country to become the 'leader of the free world'. ✪

RIGHT: President Woodrow Wilson appears before Congress announcing an official break in relations with Germany on February 3, 1917, after its ambassador informed US officials that it would not restrict submarine attacks to military targets. ✪

The First World War, President Woodrow Wilson and the League of Nations

As tensions escalated to the point of war in Europe in 1914 the US, as it had done when Britain and France collided in the 1790s, declared neutrality and insisted it could continue to trade or loan money to any of the belligerents involved.

Americans were soon caught in the crossfire however as German submarine warfare led to the deaths of US citizens in the Atlantic, including 128 civilians on board the RMS *Lusitania* in 1915. The German government conceded to President Woodrow Wilson's demands that passenger ships were off limits to attack, and this was enough to suppress any initial notion in America that the country should break with more than a hundred years of isolationism and enter the theatre of war in Europe.

By early 1917 the German military became convinced that unrestricted warfare at sea could help defeat Great Britain and because US trade with the Allies had extended to munitions and military hardware, Germany argued that America

was in fact no longer neutral. On January 31, Germany presented US Secretary of State Robert Lansing with a note declaring its intention to restart unrestricted submarine attacks the following day.

Wilson appeared in front of Congress just four days later to announce he had severed diplomatic relations with Germany, but he didn't go as far as asking for a declaration of war knowing that he lacked both public and political support to reverse US neutrality despite the deaths of numerous US seamen and citizens.

Later in the month, Wilson asked Congress for authority to arm merchant ships but was blocked by several anti-war senators which further highlighted the reluctance for America to enter the fray.

With the issue of submarine attacks ongoing, information also emerged of Germany's attempts to secure a secret alliance with Mexico and to help aid the country take back the territory it had lost to the US in the 1800s. The Zimmerman

Telegram, named after its sender the German foreign minister Arthur Zimmerman and which contained details of Germany's plot, was intercepted by the British and passed to the Americans. It sparked outrage in the US and marked the first time a major European power had made a genuine attempt to contravene the Monroe Doctrine and involve itself in the Americas.

Along with the continued sinking of US ships and Germany's apparent lack of interest in a peaceful resolution, public opinion finally swayed in favour of war and the president asked Congress for a formal declaration. American involvement ultimately helped secure a victory for the Allies as Germany offered its surrender in 1918, but the US was never actually tied to any nation by a formal alliance during its

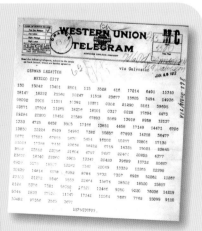

The telegram which was sent by German foreign minister Arthur Zimmerman to the President of Mexico, via the German ambassador, proposing a military alliance against the US. In return for its support, Germany would help Mexico regain New Mexico, Texas and Arizona. The British intercepted the secret message, deciphered it, and turned it over to the American government. ✪

The full text of the deciphered Zimmerman Telegram. ✪

This propaganda poster by artist James Montgomery Flagg presents Columbia, the personification of America, resting in a chair with her eyes closed as smoke and flames arise on the horizon. The text 'WAKE UP, AMERICA!' and 'CIVILISATION CALLS' shows feeling had shifted in sections of American society towards the US having a role to play in spreading its values of freedom across the world. ✪

TOP: The headline in the *New York Times* from April 3, 1917, as Wilson heads towards direct involvement in the First World War. ✪

MAIN IMAGE: Army recruits who answered the call to war fill a street in New York City in April 1917, shortly after Congress had ratified the declaration. *Courtesy, PA*

involvement in the First World War.

Wilson's desire to join the fight was, in practical terms, about protecting American lives and trade overseas along with securing its own borders in light of the Zimmerman Telegram, and those aims had been achieved. Unlike the presidents of the early 19th century however, Wilson was from the generation of Manifest Destiny and held an inner belief that US foreign policy should be about more than its own self-interest, defined also by ideals, morality and the spread of democracy all over the world, not just in the Americas. In early 1918, with the war still raging, he unveiled his Fourteen Points to Congress in which he put forward a vision of how the conflict could end; eight of the 14 points relating to specific territorial issues among the rival nations, and five others suggesting principles for a peaceful world.

The content was warmly received by the Allies in Europe and also had a favourable reaction in America despite it being almost completely at odds with the long-held policy of isolationism from events and

affairs outside the Western Hemisphere. It seemed, for the moment at least, that the tide had turned. With the war at an end, Wilson joined his European counterparts for a peace conference in Versailles, France, and attempted to turn his Fourteen Points into a formal treaty. Unfortunately for him, and significantly for America, he failed. The Treaty of Versailles had aspects of Wilson's vision within it, but he was forced to accept Allied demands for financial reparations from Germany, along with other punishments, which left the agreement flawed from the start.

Where Wilson did succeed was in the formation of a League of Nations – the last of his 14 statements. He believed that a collective of nations, under US leadership, could provide security in Europe and ensure that war never occurred again and although this notion achieved worldwide support its establishment proved difficult, particularly as the final Treaty of Versailles hadn't adopted the entirety of Wilson's initial vision. Despite this, Wilson was ready for America to enter the group but there was one significant issue which caused him serious difficulties: the fact that America would be compelled to come to the aid of other members that needed defence.

With the Republican Party having taken control of Congress, the Democratic president had to convince them to vote in favour of US participation and before he'd even left for France to begin negotiations Senate majority leader Henry Cabot Lodge had begun whipping up opposition.

There was support across the political spectrum in America for an international body which would work for peace and security, but the fear of conceding control of its own course to European interests proved too much and the US eventually reverted

back to its traditional isolationist position. In March 1920, the Senate voted 49-35 against involvement in both the Treaty of Versailles and the League of Nations and decided instead to sign separate peace agreements with the countries it had fought during the First World War. Wilson's insistence that the treaty be closely linked to the League of Nations only served to cement congressional opposition.

While it would take the Pearl Harbor attack to fully jolt the US back out of its isolation, Wilson's approach had a lasting impact and subsequent presidents worked far more closely with European governments, and the League of Nations itself. The organisation also inspired the subsequent formation of the United Nations.

The 'Big Four' at the Paris Peace Conference in 1919. From left to right: British Prime Minister David Lloyd George, Italian statesman Vittorio Orlando, French premier Georges Clemenceau and US President Woodrow Wilson. ✪

A political cartoon from 1919 depicts the European nations as crying babies, each with their own claims and wants, as Woodrow Wilson attempts in vain to work his Fourteen Points into the Treaty of Versailles. ✪

CHAPTER 2

THE WAR IN EUROPE

The end of American neutrality

Pearl Harbor would become a defining event of the Second World War for America, but it took place more than two years after Germany's invasion of Poland in 1939 had sparked the conflict. In the intervening period, the US had to find answers to questions of morality, finance and politics as its leaders sought the best course of action...

As America withdrew back in to isolationism following the Senate's rejection of the League of Nations, the Republicans would also take control of the White House for more than a decade after Democratic President Woodrow Wilson left office in 1921. By the time his fellow party member Franklin D Roosevelt was elected in 1933, non-interventionism was the dominant school of thought and the new president had to concentrate on dragging America out of the slump that followed the Wall Street Crash.

At the same time the fragile peace that the League of Nations had established in Europe was on the verge of collapse and it would not be long before the US would be unwillingly drawn into a second European war in 25 years.

Roosevelt's Quarantine Speech

For the entirety of the 1930s, particularly in the first half, America was preoccupied with the crippling economic turmoil which had followed the crumbling of its stock market in October 1929. The Wall Street Crash had left the US on its knees, and there were consequences all over the world. Those effects had a significant role in the rising tensions throughout Europe as many people turned their backs on the governments of the day in favour of ambitious new leaders who swept to power, sometimes by force and often on a platform of nationalism.

After brutally consolidating his rule over Germany, Adolf Hitler sought domination over the continent and began the rearmament of his military in earnest;

something which went against international law and contravened the terms of the Versailles peace treaty. America, along with Britain and France, had neither the inclination nor the strength to offer any real resistance and this only encouraged Hitler to continue as he expanded his Nazi party and set about building an empire. In Italy, Benito Mussolini's fascism movement took hold as did the nationalists in Spain led by army general Francisco Franco, who coordinated an uprising against the democratically elected government.

Concern over these developments dominated the foreign policy approach of the first Roosevelt administration but with overwhelming support for isolationism from

A British newspaper vendor holds a sign bearing a simple message: Europe is at war again. ✿

The Heinkel He 111, one of the technologically advanced aircraft designed and built in Germany during the 1930s as part of a clandestine rearmament programme, in direct violation of the Treaty of Versailles.
Courtesy, Bundesarchiv ✱

within his own government and inaction on the part of more friendly European nations, he could do nothing to intervene.

Indeed, shortly after taking office, Roosevelt proposed that he should be able to consult with other nations to place pressure on foreign aggressors in times of international conflict, but the bill ran in to strong opposition from isolationist members of the House of Representatives. Americans, politically and publicly, remained convinced that involvement in the First World War had been a mistake and hearings led by Senator Gerald Nye in 1934-35 revealed that international bankers and arms dealers had encouraged Woodrow Wilson to enter the conflict and had enjoyed significant profits which only served to harden the stance.

Republican Senator Gerald Nye who led the charge for isolationism in the American government during the interwar period. ✪

The panic and chaos caused by the Wall Street Crash is highlighted by huge crowds descending on a bank in New York. Political attention in the aftermath was focused squarely on domestic policy and away from the events of Europe. ✪

German leader Adolf Hitler, founder of the Nazi movement. ✪

Italian leader Benito Mussolini, founder of fascism. ✪

Spanish leader Francisco Franco, head of the nationalists. *Courtesy, PA*

Ho Hum! No chance of contagion.   By Dr. Seuss

A cartoon critical of isolationism by American author and illustrator Theodor Geisel, better known as Dr Seuss. Published in the early 1940s, the message invokes the Quarantine Speech by showing the dictators of Europe and their actions as diseases.

European leaders are pictured before the signing of the Munich Agreement where Hitler's expansion across the continent went unchallenged. From left to right, British Prime Minister Neville Chamberlain, French Prime Minister Édouard Daladier, Hitler, Mussolini and Italian Foreign Minister Gian Ciano. *Courtesy, Bundesarchiv* ✱

Franklin D Roosevelt, the 32nd President of the United States, in 1933 – the year he took office in his first term. ○

Peace movements spread on college campuses, too, and the growing European immigrant population in the US generally supported the rise of nationalist movements in their own countries, even when they were being driven by dictatorial governments. History was playing its part as well, and isolationists had plenty of precedent to draw upon as they invoked the words of George Washington and the other American forefathers who had advocated non-involvement in the European wars of the 19th century and had allowed the natural buffers of the Atlantic and Pacific oceans to keep them detached from the affairs of the old world.

In 1935, much to Roosevelt's dismay, US lawmakers began to pass a series of Neutrality Acts which prohibited American citizens from travelling on the ships of belligerents and the sale of arms to countries deemed to be at war. These edicts were aimed at preventing situations similar to those which had occurred prior to the First World War: Americans dying at sea as a result of German submarine attacks and German leaders rejecting American neutrality on the basis of the US supplying aid and arms to other nations. Both had been crucial to American entry into the conflict in 1917, and the isolationists would go to any lengths to prevent a repeat. Roosevelt, who had to maintain support for his domestic stimulus package known as the New Deal, had little choice but to accept.

As the decade progressed the president became more and more concerned with the actions of Hitler in Germany who had now begun his campaign against the nation's Jewish population, stripping them of their citizenship and their property and deporting them. He decided it was time to act and, in 1937, delivered what became known as the Quarantine Speech.

In it, and without referencing any individual state or person, he called for an international 'quarantine of aggressor nations' as he likened such actions of brutality to a disease.

After the conference had been concluded, Chamberlain returned to Britain and declared that the Munich Agreement meant 'peace for our time'. ✪

Churchill began secret correspondence with Roosevelt when he was a senior figure in the British Royal Navy and the two forged a close personal relationship. ✪

Initial reaction from within America saw the isolationists dig in even deeper and non-interventionists launched protests.

The media also hit back and the address was criticised in several newspapers including the *Chicago Tribune* and the *New York Sun* – the latter featuring a two-page advertisement lamenting Roosevelt which was paid for and created by famed cartoonist Percy Crosby. But, despite the vitriol, over time the stance taken in the Quarantine Speech began to gain some support and propaganda critical of isolationism began to appear.

Despite this murmuring of support for involvement in the European wars, Roosevelt had few options on the table and emphatically stated that the US would not be part of any formal alliance to stop Hitler. In Europe, appeasement prevailed and at the Munich Conference of 1938 Hitler's annexation of parts of Czechoslovakia was ratified as the leaders of Britain and France sought to avoid all-out war, hoping that Germany's expansionism had peaked.

That hope lasted a little less than a year as Germany and the Soviet Union put their differences aside to sign a non-aggression pact, allowing Hitler to invade Poland. Appeasement was no longer an option as both Britain and France, who had both pledged to protect Poland from German aggression, declared war.

German soldiers march on the Champs Élysées in Paris after occupation of the city by Hitler's forces. The news sparked anger and resentment in America, and was significant in building support for US intervention in the Second World War. *Courtesy, Bundesarchiv* ✱

Lend-Lease and military aid

The humanitarian aspects of the Second World War were crucial in swaying American public opinion towards intervention. Pictured are a group of British school pupils waving for the camera as they receive plates of bacon and eggs sent from across the Atlantic. ✪

Within a year of the outbreak of the Second World War, the Nazi blitzkrieg – against little opposition – had overrun Poland, much of Scandinavia, Belgium and the Netherlands, and by June 1940 its forces occupied Paris and dominated vast territories of North Africa.

For nearly two years before America did eventually enter the war, Britain stood against Hitler in Europe alone and vowed to repel the threat of a German invasion by all means necessary. In the Battle of Britain, 1940-1941, the Royal Air Force managed to combat a relentless offensive by the Luftwaffe which inspired British Prime Minister Winston Churchill to famously declare: "Never in the field of human conflict was so much owed by so many to so few." In another historic speech – known primarily for its line 'we shall fight on the beaches' – Churchill also made a direct plea to Roosevelt when he called on the new world to step forward with 'all its power and might' and liberate the European powers that were under siege.

The US leader believed Hitler's aggression posed a direct threat to his country, but even after the war had begun the prevalent feeling in America was still towards isolationism and the German premier actually had more than a few admirers in America who believed he would suppress the spread of communism. Even before 1939 though, Roosevelt had made moves to support Britain, France and the other Allied forces against the German onslaught. In that year he described the two European nations as America's "first line of defence" and decided that they needed American aid. To provide this, he circumvented the various neutrality acts by allowing France to make huge orders of American aircraft on a cash-and-carry basis – ensuring that money was received up front, unlike in the First World War

when it became clear the European powers did not have the funds to repay their debts. Once Germany had conquered France and installed its puppet Vichy government, Roosevelt arranged for the French orders to be delivered to the British instead.

The fall of Paris sent shockwaves across America as pro-intervention groups began to formalise and provide genuine opposition to the isolationists. In practical terms, there was support from American businesses for an increase in arms – both for its own defence and for sale – as it provided a potentially vast revenue stream only 10 years on from the Wall Street Crash, although leading military figures opposed the sale of arms and equipment, insisting that America should increase its own stockpiles instead.

With the public opposing direct military involvement, war was still not an option and so Roosevelt had to develop initiatives which complied with congressional laws, satisfied military and business leaders, and were acceptable to US citizens.

In September 1940, Roosevelt signed a 'Destroyers for Bases' agreement whereby the US provided Britain with more than

50 obsolete destroyers in exchange for 99-year leases on territory in Newfoundland and the Caribbean which would be used as US air and naval bases. Later that year, Churchill warned Roosevelt that Britain was struggling financially and could no longer purchase items on a cash-and-carry basis, forcing the US to propose a new initiative that would be known as Lend-Lease.

America would provide military supplies for the fight against Germany, but there were two caveats: the supplies would be 'lent' on the promise of payment at a later date, and payment would not come in the form of cash but instead Britain pledged to support American aims of a liberalised global economic model for the post-war world. Despite contravening the Neutrality Act, Congress approved the Lend-Lease bill in 1941, and the debate which preceded its passing also saw Roosevelt block attempts to exclude the Soviet Union from receiving US assistance. This was a significant strategic victory for the president who was convinced a Russian alliance would be crucial to defeating Germany after Hitler had reneged on his non-aggression pact with Soviet leader Joseph Stalin.

President Roosevelt signs the Lend-Lease bill into law, allowing the US to provide military equipment to countries it supported during the Second World War. ✪

The Lend-Lease memorial in Fairbanks, Alaska, which commemorates the shipment of US aircraft to the Soviet Union as part of the act.
Courtesy, jkbrooks 85 ✱

The Atlantic Charter

With military supplies and aid starting to flow from America to countries in Europe, and other nations across the world who were opposed to Hitler and the Axis powers, Roosevelt began to promote his own vision for the type of global society he wished to see develop once fighting had ended.

The situation at home was still fragile in the wake of the Wall Street Crash and the world was at war so Roosevelt made the unprecedented move of seeking a third term in office – arguing that the unpredictability of a new president could jeopardise causes both in America and abroad. He enjoyed a wide margin of victory in both the electoral college and the popular vote and finally had both the mandate and means to pursue his foreign policy aims, albeit still without support for direct US military involvement in the war.

In his 1941 State of the Union address, Roosevelt channelled Wilson's Fourteen Points to present his own Four Freedoms: freedom of speech, freedom of worship, freedom from want and freedom from fear. Having pioneered the use of mass communication methods such as radio to communicate directly with the electorate, a week prior to the Four Freedoms speech he had used one of his Fireside Chat addresses to declare that America should be the 'arsenal of democracy', and his personable and engaging approach garnered support from the people as he slowly but surely laid out the case for American intervention.

Roosevelt met Churchill in August 1941 in Newfoundland and the president's ideals for how the world would look once the conflict had ended were high on the agenda. The two drafted an agreement which included eight common principles covering issues such as free trade, worldwide welfare standards and the prevention of territorial expansion. Crucially, both leaders committed their respective countries to supporting the restoration of democratically chosen and elected forms of self-government for nations that were occupied during the Second World War.

The joint document that emerged from the meeting was the Atlantic Charter, and although not a binding treaty it was

Roosevelt and Churchill sit during a church service on board HMS *Prince of Wales* where the two were meeting to form the Atlantic Charter. ○

A sign at an anti-war protest uses the words of the third US president, Thomas Jefferson. ○

significant in establishing a sense of official solidarity between Great Britain and the US against German aggression. Most importantly though, it translated the Four Freedoms of Roosevelt into genuine Allied aims, and the president went about bolstering their support, at various times comparing them to the Ten Commandments, the Magna Carta and the Emancipation Proclamation. In a nation that was still blighted by discrimination against various sections of its own society, the Four Freedoms also gave Americans the sense that they were fighting for their own freedoms and not just those of people more than 3000 miles away across the oceans.

Roosevelt's pact with Churchill was one of the final pieces of the jigsaw as he moved closer to majority support for American involvement in the Second World War. There was certainly no neutrality as US backing came down firmly on the side of the Allies and the president had tapped in to those old dreams of Manifest Destiny with his vision of a free and democratic world. America was on the precipice but it would take something seismic to finally break the chains of isolationism. As focus continued on the events occurring in Europe, it was rising tensions and a devastating attack in the Pacific which would be the eventual catalyst for American entry.

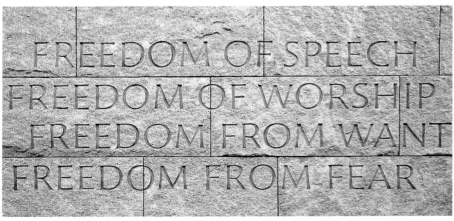

Roosevelt's Four Freedoms are commemorated at the Franklin Delano Roosevelt Memorial in Washington DC. *Courtesy, BanyanTree* ✱

CHAPTER 3

THE PACIFIC THEATRE

America, Japan and the road to war

The Japanese attack on Pearl Harbor brought the Second World War into the Pacific Theatre. The event, particularly its location, may have been a surprise but tensions between America and Japan had been simmering in the region for nearly two decades...

While European leaders Hitler, Mussolini and Franco were dismantling the peace in Europe, the domination of the Japanese empire in Asia meant America faced the escalating threat of conflict from across both the Atlantic and Pacific oceans.

As in Europe, the rise of nationalism and militarism in Japan was driven by the economic turmoil experienced during the 1920s as a result of post-First World War decline and then later the Wall Street Crash. Japan's strength lay in its status as a manufacturing and industrial power, but that meant it required huge quantities of raw materials which it simply did not possess. It therefore became dependent on the western nations as its suppliers – most notably America – with whom its own ideals and values clashed.

As a result, Japan's military leaders and Emperor Hirohito set their sights on expansion in East Asia, where resources were plentiful and could be seized with fewer strings attached. The resource-rich region of Manchuria in particular – close to the Soviet Union, China and Japan – became a key target.

At the Washington Naval Conference in 1921-1922 the US, Great Britain, Japan, France, Italy, Belgium, the Netherlands, Portugal and China had all agreed to the Nine-Power Treaty which, although acknowledging Japanese domination in Manchuria, recognised the importance for all participating nations of access to its abundant markets.

The treaty also aimed to ensure Japan would not seek further expansion in China and it succeeded, for nearly a decade, in upholding a fragile status quo.

Crucially though, because it called for further consultations rather than any punishment or sanction, when Japanese forces actually entered Manchuria its authority crumbled.

Japan invades Manchuria

Conflict in the Pacific during the Second World War began in earnest on December 7, 1941, with the Japanese attack on Pearl Harbor but its origins can be traced back to an event on September 18, 1931, known as the Mukden Incident.

On that date, a small explosion occurred on a Japanese-owned railway line in Manchuria which did so little damage it didn't even prevent a train passing across the targeted section just a few minutes later. However, the Imperial Japanese Army blamed Chinese nationalists for the 'attack' and used the incident as a pretext to launch a full-scale invasion and occupation of Manchuria which they achieved with little resistance from the untrained Chinese forces charged with defending it.

Controversy still exists today as to the identity of the assailants, with evidence suggesting the act was carried out by ambitious officers of the Japanese military who wanted to provoke conflict with the Chinese troops and take control of the region. The autonomy that existed within Japan's armed forces certainly made this possible as political leaders – and even the emperor – struggled to assert any authority over them.

Indeed, the invasion itself sent shockwaves through the political sphere in Tokyo because it had far exceeded the limitations placed on Japan but with army and navy leaders holding constitutional power in the Japanese cabinet the government could do little to oppose them. As the invading forces racked up one victory after another over the Chinese in towns and cities along the 730-mile long stretch of railway, politicians had little option but to accept and support the expansion.

The Mukden Incident may well have been staged, but, whoever laid the dynamite, the outcome was a new

Japanese experts inspect the scene of the explosion on the railway line - the source of the Mukden Incident in 1931. ✪

The raising of the Japanese flag in Manchuria stood firmly in defiance of American foreign policy and Chinese territorial integrity. ○

Japanese troops march into Mukden on September 18, 1931. ○

autonomous state in the region called Manchukuo with a puppet government controlled by the Japanese. There was now no doubt across the world as to who held power over Manchuria.

America and other western powers were deeply concerned but did not wish to become involved and took no action. Worldwide economic depression meant support for financial sanctions was almost nonexistent but America did sit in on League of Nations meetings for the first time to try and encourage the enforcement of the Kellog-Briand Pact of which Japan and China were both signatories.

The agreement, which had been finalised in Paris in 1928 was an international effort to outlaw war and prevent a repeat of the conflict which had engulfed the globe earlier in the century. The Mukden Incident and invasion of Manchuria was its first major test and although Japan had been involved in the creation of the pact, there was no means by which it could be enforced.

As the League of Nations failed in its efforts to dictate or negotiate a peace in Manchuria, US Secretary of State Henry Stimson issued what would become known as the Stimson Doctrine. This stated America would not recognise the incorporation of what had been Chinese territory into the Japanese Empire. It would also fail to recognise anything that might impair free trade in the region. Throughout the 1920s and 30s, as major cities continued

to grow on the US west coast and Pacific territories such as the Philippines, Guam and Hawaii developed under American control, trade and investment in China – and Japan – became vital to the US economy. Despite its isolationist tendencies, whenever America felt its commercial activities abroad were hindered it would swiftly embark upon a course of foreign policy intended to maintain its interests. Its approach to Asia was three-fold: the guarantee of equal access to commercial opportunities in China, the territorial integrity of China and a commitment to cooperation with other powers with interests in the region.

As the influence of the Nine-Power Treaty diminished and other diplomatic actions failed, the Stimson Doctrine was intended to pursue these American aims. In the face of continued Japanese aggression and with no desire for military engagement, however, it proved to be as ineffectual as the League of Nations.

America sent an unofficial delegate – together with a League of Nations group – to investigate the Mukden Incident and subsequent invasion and the resulting report blamed both overzealous Japanese military forces and Chinese nationalists. Importantly, it refused to recognise Manchukuo. The Lytton Commission, which produced the report, argued that the new state violated the territorial integrity of China which the Nine-Power Treaty had

protected and the League of Nations ratified its findings in 1933. In response, the Japanese delegation in Geneva walked out, never to return to the league's council, and soon after it signed a truce directly with China that maintained its full authority over Manchuria.

Alongside the signing of the Nine-Power Treaty at the Washington Naval Conference at the start of the 1920s was the Five-Power Treaty agreed by the US, Great Britain, Japan, France and Italy. It was the basis for a programme of naval disarmament by the nations which set restrictions on the warship tonnage each could possess, called for the end of capital ship building and encouraged the scrapping of older vessels. American policymakers were also forced to accept the inclusion of Article XIX which accepted US, British and Japanese bases in the Pacific but outlawed further expansion. Navy officials believed this would endanger bases in Guam, the Philippines and Hawaii, where Pearl Harbor was developing into a key strategic location.

Stimson declared that the internationally accepted Japanese violation of the Nine-Power Treaty meant the US no longer considered itself bound by the naval limitations also set out at the conference and would soon set about a rapid expansion of its forces. There now existed a set of circumstances which allowed for the potential of a naval arms race between the two major powers of the Pacific theatre.

The second Sino-Japanese War

Within Asia itself, Japan's ambitious expansion plans did not end with Manchuria. A heightened state of tension remained and after its successful conquest of the region Japan attacked the city of Shanghai in 1932.

Driven by its obsession with self-reliance, its army responded to the beating of five Japanese Buddhist monks and the burning down of a factory by concentrating some 30 ships, 40 aircraft and nearly 7000 troops around Shanghai's coastline to put down any further violence.

Arguments persist that, like the Mukden Incident, Japanese military agents orchestrated the events to give it just cause for its aggressive actions. An ultimatum was issued to the Shanghai Municipal Council demanding condemnation of the beating of Japanese monks, compensation for any property damage and action to suppress anti-Japanese protests which had broken out. On the afternoon of January 28, the council ceded to the demands.

Despite this, internal issues in China meant the nation's 19th Route Army massed outside the city causing consternation among Shanghai's officials and the foreign powers who had trade interests there. As a response, Japanese carrier aircraft began a bombing campaign in the city and 3000 troops spread quickly from the Japanese district of Hongkew to much of the Chinese-controlled areas of the city.

It would be more than two months before China and Japan signed the Shanghai Ceasefire Agreement and by that time the conflict had escalated into an international incident which saw the US and the League of Nations intervene.

While the western powers were able to broker a fragile peace in 1932, the situation was dire. Japan was intent on expansion in the region, the Chinese government was fractured, possessing little ability to resist and Japanese political leaders had little control over their nation's military; this combination of factors making further

Barbed wire fencing protects the Shanghai International Settlement as Japanese troops sweep through the Chinese-controlled areas of the city. *Courtesy, Bundesarchiv* ✱

conflict inevitable. When Japanese and Chinese forces exchanged fire – for reasons which remain a mystery – on the night of July 7, 1937, there was a stand-off between the two which came to a head on the Lugou, or Marco Polo, Bridge near Beijing. While both governments made efforts to prevent an escalation of the situation, their lack of authority over their respective militaries saw fighting intensify into a full-scale second Sino-Japanese war and within six months Japan had invaded China and assumed full control of Beijing, Shanghai and Nanjing.

Before conflict broke out and despite its close relationship with China, few US officials had advocated anything more than diplomatic protests against Japanese actions, believing that American interests in the area had not been affected enough to warrant the risk of a costly war.

As Japanese forces swept down the coast, often with brutal consequences for Chinese soldiers and civilians, the expansion

combined with the way in which it was achieved swung popular opinion in the US in favour of China and President Franklin Roosevelt formalised US aid for the country in the same way he would do for Britain and other nations in Europe.

Relations between America and Japan soured further when the Japanese army bombed the USS *Panay* as it evacuated American citizens from Nanjing, killing three of them. Roosevelt and Congress accepted an official apology and an uneasy truce held between the two held as the 1940s arrived.

During this time, the US was the main supplier of the oil, steel and iron needed by the Japanese military, especially as stubborn Chinese resistance held up its progress. This fact played its part in American reluctance to entirely oppose Japanese aggression with the country relying on this kind of income during the period after the Wall Street Crash. As Roosevelt's New Deal policies began to take hold, the sale of military hardware to the warring nations in Europe gave the US a more sound financial platform from which to express its moral opposition to what was occurring across the Pacific and when Japan revoked its treaty of commerce with America, the president had both the strength and the support to restrict the military items being supplied.

Japan's government, either incapable or unwilling to stop its military, announced

A Chinese sentry stands guard on Lugou bridge in July 1937. Fighting between Chinese and Japanese soldiers at this location would spark the second Sino-Japanese war. ✪

The US Navy river gunboat USS *Panay* in China in August 1928. ✪

As negotiations between the nations continue, Japanese ambassador Admiral Kichisaburo Nomura, left, and special envoy Saburo Kurusu, right, join US Secretary of State Cordell Hull, centre, in Washington DC on November 17, 1941. ✪

Japanese troops round up Chinese civilians in Nanjing on December 16, 1937. Many Chinese were killed during the fighting and the humanitarian crisis played a significant role in swaying American opinion from isolation to intervention. ✪

its intention to drive western imperialists from Asia so it would no longer have to rely on its trade agreements. Several pacts were then signed with western nations which placed it firmly at odds with the US; first the Tripartite Pact with Nazi Germany and fascist Italy, then a neutrality pact with the Soviet Union.

The second of these showed Japan would be moving into southeast Asia where the US had even greater trade and commercial interests, and a third agreement further fanned the flames as the Vichy government which now ruled France allowed Japanese forces to move into Indochina.

These actions were enough to prompt a full embargo and Roosevelt halted negotiations with Japanese diplomats and froze Japanese assets in US banks. The impasse was broken intermittently as officials from both nations attempted to reach a settlement but the pro-Chinese sentiment felt by Americans meant that Japanese withdrawal from China was a non-negotiable condition; one that the Imperial Japanese Army would never be willing to accept.

Roosevelt's trade embargo had left Japan running out of resources fast and with no way to scale back their military commitments in China, army leaders decided that US influence in the Pacific had to be neutralised.

With the embargo in place, military aid flowing to China and the massing of American naval forces in the Pacific, Japan – like Germany in Europe – could also argue that despite its public declarations of neutrality the US had all but entered the war already and its acts of aggression had to be met in kind.

As tensions mounted and with negotiations failing, at the end of November 1941 the US military intercepted messages revealing that a Japanese assault in the Pacific was imminent.

Page one of a US army alert order dated November 28, 1941, which was issued to military commanders on the west coast indicating the rising tensions with Japan and the continued failure of diplomatic negotiations. ✪

CHAPTER 4

The United States Navy

Conflict in the Pacific Theatre had been brewing since the early 1930s, but when Japanese forces attacked Pearl Harbor in December 1941 it wasn't the result of an isolated incident or an incendiary event but rather the outcome of careful planning and strategic thinking. The Hawaiian location was chosen with the specific aim of weakening the US Navy which had grown into one of the most powerful military organisations in the world...

America was founded on a tradition of sailing and seafaring activities and the early colonies consisted of large communities of sailors and shipbuilding industries. It's 'Old Navy' – that which existed from the start of the Revolutionary War through to the shortly after the American Civil War – played a crucial role in the eventual establishment of independence, but as the 1800s came towards a close it was clear that the US Navy was no longer fit for purpose and was in desperate need of immediate modernisation.

In 1882, Navy Secretary William H Hunt requested funds from Congress for the building of modern vessels and, after some initial wrangling, he was authorised to oversee the construction of three protected cruisers – USS *Chicago*, USS *Boston* and USS *Atlanta*. This was the start of America's 'New Navy'.

Over the course of the next 18 years, the US Navy went from the 12th largest in the world to the fifth – a period which included the building of America's first battleship, the USS *Texas*.

During that time, influential American thinker Alfred Thayer Mahan published his book, *The Influence of Sea Power upon History, 1660-1783*, which put forward the notion that countries with greater naval power will have a greater worldwide impact. As Manifest Destiny drew America across the frontier and in to the Caribbean, Hawaii and other Pacific territories, Mahan's work was influential in justifying an expanded navy as being central to the cause.

The navy's involvement in the Spanish-American War of 1898 gave reason for both celebration and concern as, although it had won several skirmishes including the Battle of Manila Bay in the Philippines, its leaders realised that if ships had been damaged or if supplies had been needed, they were 7000 miles away from the nearest American stations. In order for the US Navy to continue growing, it would need more bases across the world and an improved infrastructure to support it.

While isolationist feelings in Congress may have presented challenges to this, the good news for the navy was that it had a vociferous political supporter in the White House. In 1901, Theodore Roosevelt took office, and under his administration the navy moved into second place in terms of world standings behind only the might of the British. The president would also pursue the building of a US-controlled canal across Central America which he believed to be of significant strategic importance as it would considerably shorten the time taken for ships to travel from the Atlantic to the Pacific, or vice-versa.

Initially it appeared as though a Nicaraguan Canal would be constructed, but Roosevelt didn't believe the US would have enough influence over this region and

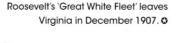
Roosevelt's 'Great White Fleet' leaves Virginia in December 1907. ✪

The USS *Texas*, the first battleship of the US Navy. ○

An aerial view of Pearl Harbor Naval Station in May 1940 shows the array of US Navy forces at the base. ○

so was able to have the decision overturned. Instead he sought to see a passage built across the Isthmus of Panama, which was controlled by Colombia.

Going through diplomatic channels at first it appeared as if the canal would go ahead but the Colombian senate failed to ratify the deal and so Roosevelt made overtures to Panamanian rebels and informed them that the US would back their cause for independence from Colombia if they revolted.

With assistance from the USS *Nashville*, authority of the area was wrestled back by Panama and on February 23, 1904, the US purchased control of the Panama Canal Zone for $10 million and now had the channel connecting the Atlantic and Pacific which was so vital to its naval development.

As his second term as president headed toward a conclusion, Roosevelt had 16 new battleships which made up his 'Great White Fleet' and to demonstrate its strength the vessels were sent on a world cruise to ports of both friendly nations and potential enemies. By this time, America had also developed its first submarine, USS *Holland*.

US involvement in the First World War hastened the building of more ships and, although the navy's direct involvement in the conflict was minimal, American leaders remained firmly behind the policy of a strong force at sea as a deterrent to future war and to secure trade interests beyond US borders. One such proponent of this was Assistant Secretary Franklin D Roosevelt.

In the early 1920s Britain, Japan and the US all began programmes to increase the size and number of their capital ships and it was the various moves and counter-moves by the three nations that led to the Washington Naval Conference. While the limitations on shipbuilding stemmed the naval arms race, one consequence of the Five-Power Treaty was the development of light cruisers and aircraft carriers, the

building of which were not prohibited. America's first carrier – the USS *Langley* – was commissioned in 1922 and was soon joined by USS *Lexington* and USS *Saratoga*.

In 1934, with growing concern about crises in Europe and Asia, Congress approved more ships and modernisation of current vessels to bring its forces up to the limits allowed. Encouragement for this came from Roosevelt, now president, who had retained his pro-navy sentiments from his days serving in the administration of Woodrow Wilson.

Once the US had decided that the Five-Power Treaty no longer applied after Japan had invaded Manchuria and established a puppet government in a new state, the naval arms race which had been halted in the early 1920s began afresh and at pace.

In 1936 America ordered its first new battleship – USS *North Carolina* – since 1921 and two congressional acts in 1937 and 1941 called for a 20% and further 11% expansion of the navy respectively.

As the potential for American entry

into global conflict became a more and more likely scenario, Roosevelt set about a rapid and complete strengthening of the navy including an increase of personnel, supplies and aircraft. In September 1940, government contracts were awarded for 210 new warships including 12 aircraft carriers and seven battleships.

By 1941, the navy had become America's most prized military asset and to many – both at home and abroad – it had now fulfilled the earlier prophecy of Mahan: the greater the navy, the greater the power of the country.

The sheer strength of the force was a daunting prospect for any would-be-aggressor, and it was growing, so in order to diminish US influence in the Pacific Theatre the US Navy would have to be significantly weakened. And, as a global identifier of American might, the fleet was a clear symbolic target for any rival nations which wanted to strike a swift and decisive blow to negate US influence in the Second World War before it officially joined the fighting.

USS *Langley*, the first aircraft carrier of the US Navy. ○

Pearl Harbor, or Pu'uloa as it was known in Hawaii, was a largely undeveloped coastal area west of Honolulu. In the late 1880s, as it became more and more likely that the island nation would become a territory of the US, navy strategists began to show an interest in the area as a possible American base. ✪

PEARL HARBOR

A US military stronghold

Hawaii joined the United States at the end of the 19th century and it was soon evident that the area known as Pearl Harbor on the northern island of Oahu would be a strategically useful location for both the US Army and Navy...

When Pearl Harbor was attacked by the Japanese Empire in 1941 it was one of the most important military bases in the US – if not the most important. As home port to the 100 vessels of the Pacific Fleet and a sizeable base for the army air services, it was crucial for the defence of America's West Coast. Just 50 years earlier, the islands of Hawaii – home to Pearl Harbor – had been in the midst of a revolution, albeit a relatively peaceful one, which had seen the monarchy overthrown by local authorities, many of whom were either American-born or descended from American business owners who had flocked to the territory earlier in the century in search of riches.

The Kingdom of Hawaii

As America experienced rapid growth in the early 19th century, its leaders used the Monroe Doctrine to assert a level of authority over all lands in the so-called Western Hemisphere. One area of interest was the Hawaiian islands which were attractive due to their involvement with the sugar industry, the whaling trade and shipping, and as early as 1820 the US appointed an official to oversee its business interests in the Port of Honolulu.

Many American citizens went to live there and became prominent figures in business and government circles. In the 1820s and 30s, many of America's growing collection of warships visited Honolulu and the US government on the mainland often sent messages of advice on how the island nation should develop its relationships with other foreign powers. A Hawaiian newspaper would later advocate that the US establish a naval base there for the protection of American citizens in the whaling business.

Once it became clear that America would eventually stretch across the continent to the west coast, the Pacific territories became even more strategically important and would be used to open up trade relationships with countries in Asia.

Lorrin Thurston, one of the Americans behind the overthrow of the Hawaiian monarchy. ○

The US Navy's Pacific Squadron was sent to explore the area, and during this survey America claimed Midway Island.

It was Hawaii itself that the officials and business owners living there really wanted, however. They viewed it as essential to US defence efforts in the Pacific and they wanted tariff-free sugar trade. In the 1870s, the island nation's ruler King Kalakaua came under pressure to cede the port of Pearl Harbor to the American navy but there was a lack of support from native residents. Instead, the Reciprocity Treaty of 1875 was agreed, which allowed Hawaiian sugar plantations and their American owners duty-free access to American markets for seven years. In exchange, the US controlled Ford Island, a small islet in the centre of Pearl Harbor, but once the

agreement expired it was handed back and sold to a private estate.

On January 20, 1887, the US began leasing Pearl Harbor but this caused unease among the peoples of the Hawaiian islands and a period of instability followed with serious questions asked of the monarchy. As internal unrest gathered pace, a number of the Americans living in Hawaii pushed for annexation of the territory by the US. Then Minister of the Interior Lorrin Thurston, the grandson of an America missionary, led a coup d'état against Queen Lili'uokalani – who had succeeded her childless brother King Kalakaua when he died of kidney disease in 1891.

With the safety of American citizens and property now under threat, John L Stevens, American Minister of State for Hawaii, ordered an invasion of US Marines from the USS *Boston* and two companies of US sailors. While they didn't occupy any buildings or even fire a shot, they served to intimidate the ill-equipped royalist defenders and the queen ordered her forces to surrender to avoid loss of life.

Immediate annexation was prevented by US President Grover Cleveland who ordered a full investigation into the actions of American-born diplomats and the American military for their respective roles in the effective overthrow of the monarchy. The Republic of Hawaii was formed, dominated by non-native residents, and its government campaigned to become an American territory, the rationale being that Hawaiian goods and services exported to the mainland would not be subject to American tariffs and the location was perfect for naval expansion. Once pro-expansionist William McKinley had succeeded Cleveland as president, the formal annexation could be completed and a ceremony was held on July 7, 1898 to mark the changeover of power.

America's new naval station

With Hawaii now an official US territory, work began in 1901 to make Pearl Harbor's shallow channel more suitable for larger American naval vessels, and more of them, as the Hawiaan islands' strategical importance grew. With that project progressing in the background, it was Naval Station, Hawaii, in Honolulu which was established first and that allowed the US Navy to explore islands and possible outposts in the surrounding area. A commander – John F Merry – was appointed to oversee the expansion.

Until 1908, the navy had committed the majority of its time and funds in Hawaii to developing the station at Honolulu and Congress approved the funding of several new facilities to support the operation including a smithy and foundry, housing and stables. Two major problems hindered development, however, the first being the increasing presence of other American government bureaus and departments which were putting a strain on both space and resources. The second arose when the vast vessels of the Asiatic station visited in 1904 to find that it was inadequately accommodated with dockage and water.

The decision was made to begin moving operations to a more suitable location, and in 1908 Naval Station Pearl Harbor was created and Congress sanctioned dredging of the channel and lochs to allow admittance of "the largest ships" and the building of shops and supply houses. Within a year work had begun on the first dry dock, and by 1910 four deep sea cargo ships had successfully used the new facility to deliver further construction materials.

Operations continued steadily for nearly a decade until the project reached completion in 1919 with few complications; the only major setback came in 1913 when the dry dock caved in due to unstable seismic activity – some native Hawaiians attributing this to be retribution of an angry shark god who they believed lived in caves under the site. While work was progressing on the shore, in 1917 the US government purchased Ford Island situated in the middle of the harbour, from its private owners, with plans to use the new land for joint army-navy projects in developing military aviation.

The battle for Ford Island

Ford Island was chosen as the location for the 6th Aero Squadron which was created in Honolulu in 1917 and the US Army's introduction of aviation divisions to the territory saw rapid expansion across all of the Hawaiian islands including improved transport networks and a civilian airport.

At the base itself, housing and hangars were erected in 1918 along with a supply warehouse, a machine shop, a photography laboratory and a power plant.

Even as army air operations increased however, navy officials concluded that a

Sailors from the USS *Boston* stand guard outside the Arlington Hotel in Honolulu during the overthrow of Queen Lili'uokalani. ○

The opening of Dry Dock No. 1 in 1919. ✪

An aerial shot of Ford Island taken circa 1919 shows how the new joint army and navy facility began to develop. ✪

A Naval Aircraft Factory TS-1 – this one assigned to aircraft carrier USS *Langley* – was the type of smaller aircraft which first occupied the naval aviation base on Ford Island. ✪

Hawaiian base was essential to their aims and earmarked Ford Island as the ideal location for expansion. In 1919, a naval air base at Pearl Harbor was commissioned and its officers moved to end army occupation Ford Island and claim it for sole use of the navy. US Secretary of War Newton D Baker ruled that the island should be divided equally between the branches of the armed forces and Luke Field – which had been named after First World War Medal of Honor recipient Frank Luke – was designated for joint army and navy efforts.

By January 1923, the nine officers and 55 men who made up the new naval detachment moved onto Ford Island with two Curtiss HS2L flying boats and two salvaged N-9 planes. After the relocation, the force received Naval Aircraft Factory TS-1, Felixstowe F5L, Curtiss H-16, Keystone PK-1 and Douglas DT type aircraft, followed by the addition of Vought FU, Vought VE-7 and Vought VE-9 biplanes.

Technological advancements saw some of these initial aircraft – the PK, F5L and H16 – replaced with newer and bigger models and by 1935 Luke Field could no longer handle the large bombers which had begun to dominate American military aviation production. Work soon began on a new dedicated army facility on the Pearl Harbor mainland which would be named after pioneering US Army Air Corps pilot Horace Meek Hickam.

Navy investment continued on Ford Island with the building of a boathouse, barracks, fire station and water-supply centre and in June 1936 the landing field was extended, taking it to 3000ft. Despite the extensions, Luke Field still wasn't big enough to house the rapidly growing US Army air forces and its operations were transferred to Hickam Field once construction had been completed in 1939.

Luke Field was renamed Naval Air Station Pearl Harbor and came under the sole jurisdiction of the navy which soon responded to direct presidential orders to prepare for increased operations by installing an additional barracks, a new

repair hangar, offices and a control tower. Domestic and leisure facilities such as a laundry and cinema were built also, as the number of service personnel and their families living at Pearl Harbor increased significantly.

A mere two miles away, Hickam Field's 7000ft-long runway was the only airstrip on the island of Oahu long enough for both the B-17 Fortress and B-24 Liberator – two giants of America's growing bomber arsenal. As preparation for potential hostilities gathered pace, a flight of 21 B-17 bombers arrived at Hickam from California in May 1941 and by the time of the Japanese attack in December the Hawaiian Air Force – formed a year earlier and headquartered at Hickam – consisted of 754 officers, 6706 enlisted men and 233 army aircraft.

Boeing P-26 Peashooter aircraft, on the left, and Douglas B-18 medium bombers parked at Hickam Field in January 1940. ✪

B-17 Fortress bombers fly over the main gate at Hickam Field during the summer of 1941 having been dispatched to the Hawaiian islands in May to bolster Pacific defences. ✪

The formation of Battleship Row

The onset of the Great Depression following the Wall Street Crash, coupled with the ongoing limitations imposed by the Five-Power Treaty, meant the 1920s were largely a time of austerity for Pearl Harbor and Ford Island and the base and surrounding landscape remained largely unchanged. Growing threats to peace in Europe and the Pacific, however, meant defence investment had restarted in earnest by 1934.

A mine-layer base, fleet air base and submarine base were built alongside the existing navy yard and naval district. Construction work in and around the Pearl Harbor base also provided jobs for many out-of-work Americans and initiatives of this sort were central to Roosevelt's New Deal. The continued and increasing aggression

of the Japanese Empire in South-East Asia in the 1930s prompted further overhauls as improvements were made to the entrance channel and a repair facility built which put the base on par with mainland American stations Mare Island in California and Puget Sound in the northern state of Washington. During that time the navy contracted a one-and-a-half million dollar dredging of the harbour to allow larger battleships to enter it, a turning channel around Ford Island was created and previous work had been done to create a concrete quay around the entire coastline to accommodate ship berthing.

As one of the top facilities in the US Navy and with ongoing tensions with Japan, the US held its Battle Fleet's exercises off Hawaii in 1940 and, having been stationed

on the American West Coast since 1922, the ships were ordered to positions at Pearl Harbor and the Pacific Fleet – which had originally only existed between 1907 and 1910 – was formally recreated on February 1, 1941. The Hawaiian naval station became its permanent base.

The work which had been carried out on the harbour and in the waters surrounding Ford Island made these the perfect home for the fleet's Battle Force battleships, and on December 6, 1941, the sun set on eight of the nine vessels which comprised the group – seven moored on the southeast shore and one across the channel in dry dock.

Early the next morning, shortly before 8am, the ships would be the primary target of Japan's surprise offensive.

An image from above the submarine base at Pearl Harbor Naval Station in October 1941 shows the expansion which had taken place over nearly half-a-century since the US Navy first began work on Oahu. The large building in the centre is the headquarters of the Pacific Fleet, while some of the large white fuel tanks have been camouflaged for fear of the damage which could be done if they were attacked. ✪

An aerial view of Ford Island in November 1941 shows four of the vessels which made up Battleship Row positioned at the south east shore. Moored to the north is aircraft carrier USS *Lexington* which was at sea during the attack on Pearl Harbor. ✪

CHAPTER 6

TORA! TORA! TORA!

Planning, preparation and launch

In western history, the story of what happened at Pearl Harbor has mainly been concerned with its devastating impact, the mistakes America made which allowed it to happen and how it brought the US into the Second World War. The less well known story is the intricate and disciplined Japanese planning which laid the foundations for one of the most audacious military operations ever conceived...

Five days before the final order for the attack was given – and 11 before it commenced – Japan's Kido Butai carrier battle group left the northern coast of the country and embarked on a journey to a position northwest of Hawaii ready for its combination of aircraft to launch against Pearl Harbor.

Despite what now seems like the obvious conclusion of US entry into the Second World War, all the evidence suggests that it was never the intention of this extensive Japanese force to draw America into all-out conflict in the Pacific – in fact, it was quite the opposite.

Without access to US oil and materials – and without comfortable military control over resource-rich areas of Asia – there was no way Japan could sustain a successful global military engagement for more than a few years. It was already feeling the strain of its commitments in China, but unwilling to pull back and appear as if it had backed down to the US there were only two alternatives – reach a negotiated settlement which saved face or push America into retreat.

Japan's chosen means of achieving the second of these was a surprise strike against the US Navy in the Pacific which would deliver such a telling blow that even if war broke out, America's military would be so weakened and morale so deflated that a swift and decisive Japanese victory would be the only possible outcome.

Concept and origins

At the start of the 1940s, the high command of the Imperial Japanese Army made preparations to move into what it called the Southern Resource Area – the Dutch East Indies, British-controlled Malaya, French Indochina and American territory in the Philippines. Requiring a far greater quantity of natural resources than its own land could offer, the military decided this expansion was crucial to achieving the nation's vision of a far-reaching and globally powerful Japanese Empire.

Hoping to capitalise on the division in the US – namely the isolationists who were still deeply rooted within government – some military leaders believed this could be achieved without provoking America into conflict. For many of the more traditional and conservative holders of high offices, the remit of the Japanese navy would be confined to defending any colonial possessions it managed to wrestle from the western powers. There were many others who fiercely disagreed, and among them was the influential commander of the Japanese navy's Combined Fleet – Admiral Isoroku Yamamoto.

He feared that Japanese operations in the Philippines would draw the US into war and, having been educated in America and having worked in the country as a diplomat, he was well aware of the huge and untapped

First wave aircraft prepare to launch against Pearl Harbor. This moment is the result of more than a year of careful planning, preparation and training. ✪

Admiral Isoroku Yamamoto pictured at an Imperial Japanese Navy planning meeting in the early 1940s. ✪

industrial machine on which it could draw during a possible conflict. Convinced by this, Yamamoto supported using Japanese naval might to launch a far more aggressive and pre-emptive strike against America in the Pacific which would disable the US fleets in the region long enough to allow Japan to exert full control over the territory it so desired.

Pinpointing the exact moment an attack on Hawaii was considered a genuine prospect within the Japanese military is difficult, and it certainly didn't carry a great deal of weight until backed by Yamamoto. Indeed, the Pacific Fleet wasn't officially moved there until May of 1940 so it's unlikely that a concrete strategy was in place before this time. There is evidence to suggest, however, that the first murmurings of such a move began as early as the 1920s, although at this stage it was nothing more than conjecture and hypothesis.

Perhaps, though, a young naval officer named Yamamoto had heard whisperings of the idea; perhaps he'd had conversations on the subject; perhaps the initial seed had been planted. Perhaps it was none of these, and Yamamoto himself conceived and developed the entire attack, but whatever influences he may or may not have drawn upon by spring of 1940 he was – albeit informally – devising a carrier-based attack against US military forces stationed at the Pacific island.

One of the key events which prompted him to formally present the plan was the Japanese fleet's naval air exercises of 1939-1940. Owing to Yamamoto's own insistence on developing the country's air power at sea, the fleet demonstrated significantly increased capabilities in this regard during training and manoeuvres and of particular

High-ranking Japanese navy officers visit the Tomb of the Unknown Soldier in Arlington, Virginia, with Captain Isoroku Yamamoto at the far right of the delegation. Yamamoto's time spent in the United States of America gave him a unique perspective on the tactical and strategic planning of a potential Pacific conflict. ✪

interest to the admiral was a simulated raid on harbour-based warships by torpedo-armed bombers.

Senior navy officers weren't convinced, but Yamamoto believed it to be a resounding success and it helped to convince him that – as long as the element of surprise was achieved – it was possible for this kind of attack to succeed in defeating the US before war had even begun.

Later in 1940, on the night of November 11 and the early hours of November 12, British naval forces launched the first ever operation of this kind as torpedo bombers of the HMS *Illustrious* struck the Italian battle fleet while it was moored in the southern harbour of Taranto. On a much smaller scale than Pearl Harbor would eventually

be, the overwhelming success of the operation saw the destruction of one Italian battleship and heavy damage sustained by two more. Admiral Cunningham, the British naval officer who oversaw the operation, said: "Taranto, and the night of November 11-12, 1940, should be remembered for ever as having shown once and for all that in the Fleet Air Arm the navy has its most devastating weapon."

While Yamamoto's plan was already under way by the time of Taranto, it seems highly unlikely that he and the Imperial Japanese Navy generally would not have studied the operation as much as possible as they formulated their own strategy for a carrier strike. In fact, Lieutenant Commander Takeshi Naito – the assistant naval attaché to Berlin – flew to Taranto to investigate first-hand, and a Japanese military mission also visited the harbour in May 1941 for discussions with members of the Italian navy.

Yamamoto was fundamentally against war with the United States, but knowing it was inevitable that the two great powers of the Pacific would collide he would do everything in his power to ensure victory for Japan. He knew his carrier attack plan had risks, but while this was still causing some concern for him by the end of 1940, the potential he saw in the fleet combined with the success the British had achieved in Taranto was perhaps what convinced Yamamoto that the high risks were worth the potential rewards.

The mighty US Pacific Fleet being moved to Hawaii not only cemented his theory that a pre-emptive strike was the only way Japan could hope for victory, but also meant a key enemy target was in a much more vulnerable location for his carrier group to attack.

On January 7, 1941, Yamamoto put his ideas on paper, sending a memo to Navy Minister Oikawa Koshiro simply titled Gumbi ni kansuru shiken – Views on military preparations.

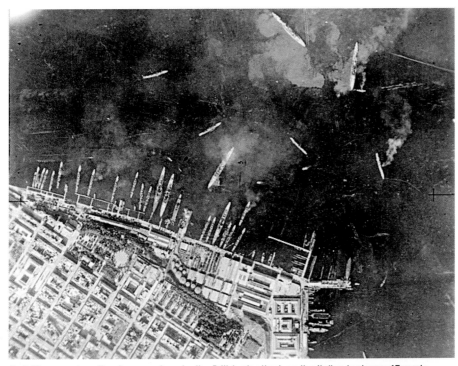
Aerial images show the damage done by the British air attack on the Italian harbour of Taranto including premier Italian battleship *Littorio* surrounded by salvage tugs. The success of this operation gave impetus to Yamamoto's notion of a carrier-based strike against the US having potential in the waters of the Pacific Ocean. ✪

Admiral Takijiro Onishi was responsible for preliminary investigations into the feasibility of Yamamoto's plan. ✪

Yamamoto's vision takes shape

Minoru Genda, centre of the three seated pilots, was an important figure in the planning and execution of the Pearl Harbor attack. ✪

While the initial plan had enough support to make it worthy of consideration, it soon became clear that Yamamoto would face two major obstacles: the ardent belief of the naval general staff that operations should be limited to defence of territorial expansion, and the fact Japan lacked the air power required to launch a strike such as the one he had proposed.

As Yamamoto's plan gained backers, it was still official navy strategy to prepare for a war with the US which would see the Japanese navy wait for American aggression as it came to the aid of either its own or Allied territory in the Pacific, and then counter-attack. Protection of the Southern Resource Area was Japan's first and foremost concern.

To see his grand vision bear fruit, Yamamoto would have to demonstrate beyond doubt that it could work and he would have to win backing from key navy figures to turn the tide of opinion against him. First, he discussed his idea with Admiral Takijiro Onishi – chief of staff of the Eleventh Air Fleet – and requested that he study its technical feasibility. His opinion: difficult, but not impossible.

Looking for further support, Onishi summoned Commander Minoru Genda – a respected naval aviator and Japanese diplomat who was a long-time associate of Yamamoto. Genda concurred with Onishi's findings, and further stressed the importance of the shock element of the attack, telling Yamamoto that 'secrecy is the keynote and surprise the all-important factor'.

Following Yamamoto's direction, Onishi, Genda and Rear Admiral Ryunosuke

Kusaka set about putting a full strategic operation into action and began training the necessary forces. It was down to Yamamoto to deal with the politics.

Well in to the summer of 1941 – with preparations under way – he was still in heated debate with the navy general staff. Not only did they lack faith in the overall plan, but considered that putting it into action would take vital resources away from the invasion of territories in Southeast Asia; the biggest point of contention was Yamamoto's desire to use at least four carriers, some of which were already reserved because the limited range of Japanese fighters meant they couldn't reach and return from the intended targets without carrier assistance.

By October, Yamamoto's persistence and persuasiveness had paid dividends as the navy general staff appeared to be close to signing off on the details of his ambitious plan which had now been formulated by Genda and Kusaka.

Helping his cause was an agreement between the branches of the Japanese military regarding the simultaneous attacks on the Philippines and Malaya which relieved some strain on the navy. The launch of two new carriers, *Shokaku* and *Zuikaku*, also eased concerns.

Just to consolidate support, Yamamoto secretly spread word to high command that if his plan were to be rejected he would resign. As a decorated naval officer, highly respected public figure and popular government advocate, the general staff

could not risk causing such unrest and had little choice but to give in.

Given the green light, Yamamoto pressed ahead but later in the month he would be back in the midst of disagreement with the general staff as he demanded the use of six out of eight Japanese aircraft carriers. He argued that the success of the venture depended on overwhelming air power. Incensed by his intention to commit such huge resources to a single attack, the general staff might have pulled the plug on the Pearl Harbor operation permanently had it not been for the fact that Yamamoto's attempts to tackle his second big problem were reaping rewards.

While it had taken a great deal of bureaucratic wrangling to, almost, overcome opposition to his plan, he was able to approach the deficiencies in Japan's naval air power to complete such a task with much more practical methods and, using his considerable influence, he directed significant time and resources to expanding and improving the force. Japan would not likely to able to match the quantity of American or British military might, but it could compete on quality.

Just when it appeared as if the operation might fall through, one such improvement – engine adjustments to the Mitsubishi A6M Zero fighter – meant the aircraft was capable of providing air cover for the forces involved in the southern operations without needing carriers to get it there.

The two major obstacles to Operation Hawaii had now been removed.

From left to right, carriers *Akagi*, *Kaga* and *Shokaku* were among the ships of the Japanese fleet. As his final plan came together, Yamamoto insisted on using six carriers as part of his Pearl Harbor strike force. ✪

Yamamoto's plan comes to life

A group portrait of the fighter squadron from carrier *Shokaku*, in front of a Zero fighter. Taken in October or November 1941, it's highly likely this group would have been training for the Pearl Harbor attack – even if they didn't know it at the time. ✿

As he employed all of his diplomatic skill and political influence to overturn two decades of Japanese naval strategy, Yamamoto had to simultaneously consider how such an ambitious endeavour – one that was fraught with challenges and risks – could actually be put in to place.

For this aspect, Yamamoto turned to Genda. Gradually, Genda developed solutions to two of the major issues: executing successful torpedo attacks in shallow waters and making level bombing against battleships worthwhile. He pursued the development of the navy's weapons which led to the introduction of modified torpedoes and armour-piercing bombs.

Genda was also responsible for training, a crucial element given that the Pearl Harbor attack was so unprecedented and on such a large scale. Over the summer of 1941, he used Kagoshima City on the island of Kyushu, deciding that the location would present many of the same geographical obstacles and a similar infrastructure to what would be encountered in Hawaii.

In training, crews had to navigate the 5000ft high mountain before diving into the city – avoiding buildings and smokestacks – before dropping down even further at the piers.

There is little doubt that the attention to detail Genda gave to the training and the plan was significant in helping Yamamoto successfully sway the general staff, and the commander also had a great deal of influence over the final objectives as the specifics of the attack came together.

Yamamoto, whose main aim was to hit America so hard that war was avoided, believed battleships should be the primary target. In his eyes, these capital vessels were the most prized asset of a navy and their destruction would have the most impact in the eyes of the public. Genda, seeing more and more how critical air power was becoming to warfare, realised the importance of aircraft carriers and was adamant that if all else failed it was these ships of the Pacific Fleet which should be destroyed.

As was always going to be the case, the destruction of carriers and battleships were both major objectives, but the weight given to the former demonstrated the respect that Genda commanded. Yamamoto may well have been the architect, but without Genda to draw up the blueprint it may never have got off the ground!

One element of the attack that Genda could not implement though was his belief that the strike should be rolled into the expansion operation in South East Asia; he wanted Japan to invade Hawaii itself.

Believing that the Pacific territory would be of huge significance in a war with the US he suggested that a force of 10,000-15,000 would be enough to assume control. Not only could Japan negate American influence by claiming Hawaii, but it could use its bases to threaten the American west coast

and possibly force a surrender or retreat. The idea wasn't rejected out of hand, but Combined Fleet Commander Yasuji Watanabe estimated that the manpower required would be three times more than Genda had reckoned, and it would need a further 80 ships to succeed.

A carrier attack was deemed risky enough, and with limited Japanese resources spread thinly in China and about to be spread further, any notion of an invasion was soon rejected.

Another part of the reason for not going ahead with an invasion effort was that Yamamoto had done such a comprehensive job of shifting opinion in favour of the idea that a massive strike would be enough to force a negotiated settlement.

With the details and military objectives of the operation coming together under the guidance of Genda it was back to Yamamoto to ensure the most important aspect of the entire plan: maintaining secrecy.

Covering up the dramatic change in general naval strategy and the preparations for the attack would be difficult enough, but moving a strike force comprising six aircraft carriers to a position close enough from which to launch was perhaps the most audacious part of the entire affair.

To achieve all of this, Yamamoto would have to exert influence over all branches of a military that was notoriously difficult to control. Perhaps only a man of his stature and standing possessed such a capability.

In November 1941, Japan began a denial-and-deception radio communications campaign aimed at duping the Americans – who were known to be monitoring its transmissions – into believing it was business as usual. Using a planned naval exercise as a ruse, Japan was able to 'hide' carrier radio communication in what was believed to be the noise of the training and when the carriers went silent in the aftermath, the US had no reason to be suspicious as the vessels had generally been quiet as they sat waiting in Japanese home waters as part of their defensive duties.

Little did they know that Kido Butai had now embarked on its voyage into history.

The force still had to arrive undetected however, and that feat would take extensive planning, intelligence gathering and sophisticated communication. From early in the preparations for Pearl Harbor, a Japanese agent in Hawaii – Takeo Yoshikawa – was gathering information on Pacific Fleet activity in the region. His reports on air force operations were limited however, so radio intelligence became vital in ensuring the element of surprise.

Crucially, it was this intelligence gathering which uncovered the severe lack of American aircraft reconnaissance to the north of Hawaii, with operations instead concentrated in the south and to the west. Resource was a problem, but it's most likely that US strategists were so confident in their assessment that Japanese naval operations were concerned with the defence of southern territories that attack from the north was almost inconceivable.

On November 5, the Combined Fleet's Operations Order No. 1 was secretly delivered to senior officers and six days later Vice Admiral Chuichi Nagumo – commander of the First Air Fleet and the man given overall command of the Pearl Harbor strike force at sea – received his final instructions.

Hitokappu Bay in the Kurile Islands was chosen as the rendezvous point for the six carriers, two battleships, two heavy cruisers, one light cruiser, nine destroyers, three submarines and eight tankers and supply ships which comprised the group.

In an effort to ensure the utmost secrecy, only at this point did details of the attack begin to filter down to those who would carry it out. Strict radio silence was to be observed and main shipping lanes avoided; the force was sailing into the unknown, either to return as heroes or fall into an American trap.

The advance elements, including the carriers, departed Hitokappu on November 26 for a position north of Hawaii.

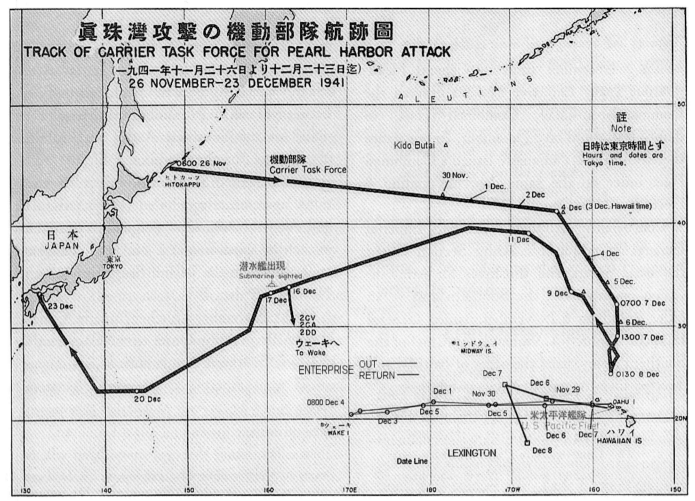

真珠灣攻擊の機動部隊航跡圖
TRACK OF CARRIER TASK FORCE FOR PEARL HARBOR ATTACK
（一九四一年十一月二十六日より十二月二十三日迄）
26 NOVEMBER–23 DECEMBER 1941

ALEUTIANS

Kido Butai △

註
Note
日時は東京時間とす
Hours and dates are
Tokyo time.

0800 26 Nov
ヒトカップ
HITOKAPPU
機動部隊
Carrier Task Force

30 Nov.
1 Dec.
2 Dec
4 Dec (3 Dec. Hawaii time)

日本
JAPAN
東京
TOKYO

11 Dec
4 Dec
5 Dec.
9 Dec
0700 7 Dec
6 Dec.
1300 7 Dec

23 Dec

潜水艦出現
Submarine sighted

16 Dec
17 Dec

2CV
2CA
2DD
ウェーキへ
To Wake

ミッドウェイ
MIDWAY IS.

ENTERPRISE
OUT ————
RETURN ———

0130 8 Dec

Dec 7
Dec 6
Nov 29
Dec 1
Nov 30
Dec 5
Dec 5
0800 Dec 4
Dec 3
ウェーキ
WAKE I

米太平洋艦隊
U.S. Pacific Fleet
OAHU I
Dec 6
Dec 7
ハワイ
HAWAIIAN IS

20 Dec

LEXINGTON
Dec 8

Date Line

130 140 150 160 170E 180 170W 160 150

50
40
30
20N

A map showing the movement of the Japanese carrier group in the Pacific en route to the attack and after it. Also shown are the movements of US carriers *Enterprise* and *Lexington* which were at sea away from Pearl Harbor at the time. ✪

Vice Admiral Chuichi Nagumo, overall commander of the Pearl Harbor strike force. ✪

The order to attack

The strike force was formidable. At this time, Japan was one of just a handful of countries even capable of carrier aviation and the Kido Butai was stronger than any other similar group in the world.

Flagship carrier *Akagi* was joined by *Kaga*, *Soryu*, *Hiryu*, *Shokaku* and *Zuikaku* – the six boasting 135 Zero fighters, 171 Nakajima B5N Kate level and torpedo bombers and 108 Aichi D3A Val dive-bombers between them. The 359 aircraft comprised the greatest concentration of naval air power ever assembled.

With this armada en route, the order came on December 1, 1941, from Imperial Japanese Navy Chief of Staff Osami Nagano and was passed to Yamamoto: "Japan has

decided to open hostilities against the United States, United Kingdom and Netherlands." The admiral was told to direct the Kido Butai to its agreed destination where it would 'launch a resolute surprise attack on and deal a fatal blow to the enemy fleet' on the commencement of hostilities.

As the fleet steamed east across the Pacific, significant low cloud cover aided their efforts to avoid detection by any patrolling American aircraft. The cloud, however, brought with it storms and as the ships moved to a position of about 1000 miles north of Hawaii a sudden storm left them scattered across hundreds of miles of open water. Using just short-range, low-power radio to communicate, the fleet

Val dive-bombers await the order to take off from carrier *Akagi*. ✪

From on board Japanese carrier *Zuikaku*, *Kaga* and *Akagi* are seen under way en route to Hitokappu Bay from where they will make their move into the Pacific toward Hawaii. ✪

A Japanese Zero fighter takes off from aircraft carrier *Akagi* to embark upon the Pearl Harbor attack. Rapid development in the months before the attack made this one of the most formidable fighter aircraft in the world. ✪

First wave aircraft, on their way south to Oahu, launch from carrier *Shokaku*. ✪

managed to regroup; a remarkable feat of navigational skill.

From December 4-6, the strike forced moved south and, by the early hours of December 7, had reached a staging point just a few hundred miles north of Oahu.

In Washington DC, just a few hours before the attack would begin, the Office of Naval Intelligence placed all of Japan's fleet carriers in home waters. Nagumo and Yamamoto wouldn't know until their aircraft broke through the clouds just tens of miles off the coast of Hawaii, but their approach had gone completely undetected. One of, if not the, most ambitious and daring raids in the long history of naval warfare was about to commence.

With no breakthrough in negotiations between the nations forthcoming, the attack was set to proceed as planned. However, on December 6, Nagumo received intelligence that the US aircraft carriers *Saratoga*, *Yorktown*, *Lexington* and *Enterprise* were all absent from Pearl Harbor and would not be returning before the morning. For all the careful plotting that went into the preparation, this was a major intelligence blunder which left question marks over whether the operation would even commence.

The carriers had become such a key objective that had the information been

revealed earlier it may well have altered the course of history but, with just hours remaining before the planned launch and the fact that Japan had already committed the vast Kido Butai to such a vulnerable position, there was no turning back. Japan knew that Battleship Row was fully occupied, and inflicting as much devastation on these American capital ships as possible would now be its main aim.

At 6.10am the first wave of 89 Kates, 51 Vals and 43 Zeros roared into the air led by Commander Mitsuo Fuchida; the incredible sight of this massive force lifting off the decks of six carriers must count among the most impressive spectacles in naval history.

As the 183 aircraft approached they were spotted by a radar operator stationed on the northern tip of Oahu who reported seeing an unusually large blip on his screens which he interpreted as a significant number of aircraft, about 132 miles away and fast approaching Oahu.

First Lieutenant Kermit A Tyler was on temporary duty in Honolulu's Fort Shafter but, knowing that a flight of US B-17 bombers were scheduled to arrive at Hickam Field around 8am, his response was: "Don't worry about it."

Congressional reports later cleared Tyler of any blame; he was an observer-trainee

in the radar room, a flight of B-17s was on approach at the time and the initial radar operators made no mention of the fact they believed the blips amounted to more than 50 aircraft which would have set alarm bells ringing. Instead, the first wave continued and it wouldn't be until first visual contact that their presence in the skies over Pearl Harbor was known. As Fuchida and his attack groups followed their training to the letter and descended on Oahu, he sent the message 'to, to, to' which was the signal to commence the attack.

Realising that the US forces based there were completely unprepared for them, he shortly followed that with the signal designated to declare the success of a surprise offensive – 'to ra, to ra, to ra'.

There has been some debate regarding what was meant by 'to ra'; the literal translation of the word tora in Japanese is tiger and pilots certainly interpreted the codename for the order to attack in this way. Many others suggest that it was an acronym for totsugeki raigeki which means 'lightning attack' – and initial use of 'to, to, to' certainly supports this.

Over time, however, perhaps because of its more poetic impact, it is Tora! Tora! Tora! – Tiger! Tiger! Tiger! – which has become the most commonly used phrase.

Carrier *Kaga* is pictured in heavy seas during its Pacific voyage. ✪

Crews of Kate bomber aircraft pose aboard *Kaga* on December 6, left. Those crews are then briefed by Lieutenant Ichiro Kitajima, above. ✪

CHAPTER 7

JAPAN'S SUPREMACY IN THE SKIES

An aerial arsenal to rival all others

As the fighting of the Second World War intensified the British RAF, German Luftwaffe and US Army and Navy air forces would move aviation technology on at a rapid rate producing some of the finest military aircraft the world has ever seen. In 1940-1941, however, for a few short years it was Japan at the forefront. With a majority of resources directed towards achieving success in its Pacific operations, the Imperial Japanese Navy had developed three aircraft types which had been perfected for the sole aim of meeting the objectives of the Pearl Harbor attack...

Nakajima B5N
Allied reporting name: Kate

The B5N Kate was the standard carrier level and torpedo bomber of the Japanese Imperial Navy in the years before the Pearl Harbor attack and was selected to drop its payloads against the primary targets moored along Battleship Row.

Originally developed in 1935 by Nakajima's Katsuji Nakamura, the Kate was seen as being nearly obsolete by 1941 attack but its capabilities were more impressive than those of its counterparts in the Allied forces and in the hands of well-trained and capable Japanese pilots it could wreak havoc.

As part of a well-coordinated attack, and afforded a suitable fighter escort, it could deliver the firepower needed to destroy capital vessels – which is exactly what it achieved on December 7.

It was also instrumental in the sinking of American carriers USS *Yorktown*, USS

A Kate in flight over Kaneohe Naval Station during the Pearl Harbor attack. ✪

Capable of carrying bombs and torpedoes, a Kate takes off from a Japanese vessel. ✪

Lexington and USS *Hornet* later in the Pacific conflict.

The subsequent B6N eventually replaced it on the front line, but the B5N which had

such impact against the Pacific Fleet in 1941 continued to serve throughout the Second World War as a training aircraft and for some anti-submarine missions.

Aichi D3A
Allied reported name: Val

The initial tests of the D3A Navy Type 99 dive-bombers were met with disappointment by the Imperial Japanese Navy, and it took a modification to its design for it to be pressed into service. Aichi won the contract over the rival Nakajima D3N and began production in December 1939.

As the new D3A1 played a small role in combat from land bases against China, trials were ongoing aboard carriers and in 1941 the aircraft took part in its first major operation: the Pearl Harbor attack.

The success it enjoyed in Hawaii, and in subsequent Japanese operations in the Pacific, made it one of the most feared sights for Allied seamen.

Its fighter-like aerial capabilities combined with unerring bombing accuracy caused devastation and the Val is credited with sinking more Allied warships in the

Second World War than any other Axis-power aircraft.

In the latter years of the conflict, however, Allied technology caught up as logistical and financial issues caused delays to planned Japanese upgrades. By 1944, when the Vals suffered heavy losses to American forces in the Philippines, the aircraft was outdated and obsolete but did make a return to combat in 1945 for kamikaze missions.

Vals were predominantly launched from carriers, but early in the aircraft's development it operated as a land-based bomber. ✪

A D3A of Japanese carrier *Akagi* in flight. ✪

Mitsubishi A6M

Allied reporting name: Zero

For a period of about 18 months – a time during which the Pearl Harbor attack took place – Japan possessed one of the most feared and dominant fighter aircraft the world has ever seen.

Four years before, as the nation prepared for expansion in South East Asia, the word was sent out from the Imperial Japanese Navy to aviation industry giants Nakajima and Mitsubishi that a new advanced fighter was required; one capable of outmanoeuvring and outpacing anything that any other country had to offer.

The precise requirements for this super-machine were: a top speed of more than 350mph at 4000m, along with the ability to climb to 3000m in just three-and-a-half minutes and a take-off run of just 70m.

Nakajima's development team believed it to be an impossible task and withdrew from consideration for the contract immediately, while Mitsubishi – having committed significant time and resource to a Japanese navy bomber project – considered turning its back, too.

However, designer Jiro Horikoshi was convinced he could achieve what many believed could not be done, and so Mitsubishi negotiated an end to the bomber development and concentrated efforts on the fighter concept.

The result was the Type 0 Carrier Fighter which commonly became known in Western circles as the Zero. The technical marvel was more advanced than anything America or Britain possessed.

Imperial Japanese Navy pilots hailed the Zero as the most efficient aircraft they had

ever flown, and its potential was showcased when it was first used in combat in August 1940 – 12 of the new fighter escorting a bombing mission against the Chinese capital.

A month later a group of Zeros shot down 27 Chinese-piloted I-15 and I-16 fighters while escorting another bombing mission, and by the end of the first year they were used in combat they had accounted for 99 Chinese aircraft for the loss of just two – both falling victim to anti-aircraft fire rather than in air-to-air combat.

Japanese navy officers believed the Zero to be an invincible flying machine and suggested that each plane was capable of fending off anywhere between two and five enemy fighters in battle.

As the aircraft developed, the third design – Model 21 – was built with folding wingtips to allow more efficient carrier use, along with an increase from a 320-litre to a 520-litre fuel tank. Now evolved for carrier missions and capable of operating at greatly increase range, the Zero was a fearsome opponent which could reach speeds of 331mph and climb to 6000m in seven-and-a-half minutes.

Its reputation meant it was the obvious weapon of choice for the Pearl Harbor attack, but such was its supremacy that only 108 of the 400 fighters available at the time were utilised. This force of Zeros was more than adequate, as it took control of the skies over the Hawaiian island for nearly two hours on the morning of December 7, allowing the bombers to rain down their devastating arsenal.

It retained its dominance for the first

US forces on Oahu did manage to account for nine downed Japanese Zero fighters during the Pearl Harbor offensive, one of the earliest signs that this fearsome foe had its weaknesses. ○

six months of the Pacific War; in the first three, Zeros had claimed an incredible 471 kills out of 565 enemy aircraft which were shot down. However, it soon became clear that significant sacrifices had been made to obtain the Zero's superior performance capabilities and they were to be its undoing.

Made out of a lightweight duralumin alloy for maximum manoeuvrability, durability under fire was given far less consideration. Armour plating was deleted from the original blueprint to cut down weight, as were the self-sealing fuel tanks which would have prevented leaks. This combination left the Zero extremely susceptible to damage caused by machine gun and anti-aircraft fire.

Initially, enemy forces couldn't exploit this because they engaged in traditional dogfighting; the Zero more than able to claim victory in such combat. Slowly, as tactics adapted, it became clear that if pilots got above the Zero and descended quickly with a short and accurate burst of fire they would almost certainly do fatal damage.

It didn't take long for other air forces to catch up, either, and by 1943 the Zero was falling behind the US-produced Grumman F6F Hellcat, Vought F4U Corsair and Lockheed P-38 Lightning fighters.

Delays to the production of new designs in Japan as the war progressed meant the Zero remained on the front line and was the most-produced Japanese aircraft of the conflict. Despite its deficiencies, it was for a brief period the ultimate fighter aircraft and has become a legend in aviation history.

The original A6M2 Type 0 Model 11 in flight over China in May 1941. ○

CHAPTER 8

TIME LINE

Key moments of the attack

December 7, 1941
Pearl Harbor
Hawaii

0743

Commander of the Japanese air-attack Mitsuo Fuchida arrives at Pearl Harbor with the first wave of the attack. The force consists of 49 level bombers, 51 dive-bombers, 40 torpedo bombers and 43 fighters. Fuchida orders his telegraph operator to tap out 'to, to, to' – the code for attack – followed by 'to ra, to ra, to ra' – the code for attack, surprise achieved. Some Japanese pilots read 'to, ra' as 'tora' which translates as 'tiger'.

0745

The attack commences as dive-bombers strike the US Army Air Force bases of Wheeler Field – north of Pearl Harbor and Hickam Field on Ford Island. Aircraft have been parked wingtip-to-wingtip in neat rows to guard against sabotage and so are easy targets.

0758

At Ford Island's Command Center, Commander Logan C Ramsey sees a low-flying plane and assumes it's a showboating US pilot. Once he realises it's enemy aircraft he runs to the radio room and orders the telegraph operators to send out a message to every ship and base: "AIR RAID ON PEARL HARBOR x THIS IS NOT DRILL".

0810

A Japanese bomber drops an armour-piercing weapon which hits the battleship USS *Arizona* setting off more than one million pounds of explosive ordnance on board. A huge fireball rips through the vessel and within nine minutes it is on the bottom of the harbour.

U. S. NAVAL COMMUNICATION SERVICE
U. S. S. WASP

Norfolk Navy Yard—12-17-40—39,939

7 DEC '41   JR

NSS ... 2 0F2 1035 0F3 0F4 1F0 0

URGENT

AIRRAID ON PEARLHARBOR X THIS IS NOT DRILL

#a INCOMING RADIO

TOR: 1936/TW/17.8
TOR: 1936 SHIPS TIME

CAPT NOTIFIED
EXEC NOTIFIED

From:	Action To:			Info. To:	STATION FILE
COM PACIFIC FLT	COMATLANTIC FLT COMASIATIC FLT OPNAV				Release
Capt.	Air.	1st Lt.	Sup.	CWO	Chap.	Duty Cdr.
XO	Gun.	Nav.	Med.	OOD	AXO	
Comm.	Eng.	Radio	Marine	Ship Sr.	Ship Sec.	

0840 |

The second wave of the Japanese attack appears in the skies, comprising 54 bombers, 78 dive-bombers and 35 fighters.

0850 |

With Pearl Harbor under siege, USS *Nevada* attempts to head for the open sea but aircraft from the second wave bomb her. Rather than risk sinking in the narrow channel, the vessel is deliberately grounded off Hospital Point.

0854 |

The Japanese force is now coming under heavy US anti-aircraft fire but is still able to target the dry dock where it hits the battleship USS *Pennsylvania*.

0930 |

A bomb blows up the bow of destroyer USS *Shaw*, with pieces of the ship from the resulting explosion raining down half-a-mile away.

1000 |

The Japanese fighters follow the bombers back to the aircraft carriers of the Japanese strike force, bringing the devastating assault to an end.

Mary Maiden of New York City, serving as a hostess at Hickham Field, witnessed this column of black smoke rising over Pearl Harbor Naval Station. She would later say that she thought a US plane had crashed into a fuel or oil depot, and she took this photo not yet having left her room after being awakened by the explosions. Courtesy, PA

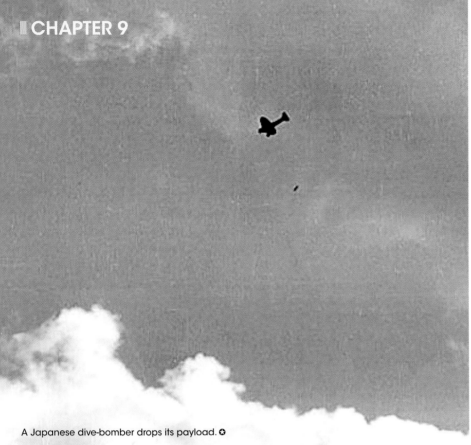

CHAPTER 9

A Japanese dive-bomber drops its payload. ✪

NEUTRALISING US AIR FORCES

The first wave begins

A crucial element to the success of the Pearl Harbor attack would be ensuring American aircraft would not have the chance to mount a defence by launching forces and engaging in aerial dogfights...

It was shortly before 8am on Sunday, December 7 – just as preparations were being made for the eight o'clock raising of the colours – when the Japanese attack against Pearl Harbor began. Warnings of a Japanese offensive had been issued in the preceding weeks and months but few expected it to take place in Hawaii.

Some 183 planes comprised the first wave and among them were 51 Aichi D3A Val dive-bombers of the attack group number two and 43 Mitsubishi A6M2 Zero fighters of attack group three whose primary targets were aircraft of both the US Army and Navy. The initial attack also included 89 Nakajima B5N2 Kate bombers but, while some did drop loads on the airfields, during the first wave the primary target for these crews was Battleship Row.

The Japanese approach to its attack on American aircraft was two-fold: inflict damage serious enough to prevent the US from mobilising its air forces and fighting back, and retain control of the skies over Pearl Harbor ahead of the second wave should American pilots make any attempt at a counter-attack.

There were six assigned targets for this portion of the attack, with Hickham Field, Wheeler Field and Ford Island as the three main locations of concern. Other US military installations in Hawaii – Kanoehe Naval Station, Bellows Field and Ewa Marine Corps Station – were all secondary targets. Haleiwa airfield, which was mainly used for training purposes, was not targeted during either wave but forces based there were involved in the day's events.

Bombers and fighters swarmed overhead

By the time the alarm was raised with the message from Ford Island – "AIR RAID PEARL HARBOR x THIS IS NOT DRILL" – Japanese aircraft were well on the way to neutralising US air forces as they sought domination above Pearl Harbor.

As the second and third groups of the first wave strafed and bombed their air corps targets, many men and women stationed at the bases were just awakening on what was intended to be a routine and peaceful Sunday morning.

Instead, they arose from their slumbers to explosions, fire and smoke as dive-bombers and fighters swarmed overhead, raining down their arsenals from all angles.

The skies over Pearl Harbor dominated by Japanese aircraft, American anti-aircraft fire and flak bursts. ✪

Hangar No. 11 of Hickam Field in ruins, with destroyed aircraft in the foreground. ✪

A Japanese Zero fighter – which, along with other aircraft of the first wave, are now dominating the skies – flying above a shot-down US aircraft which burns in a field near Ewa Marine Corps Air Station. ✪

The five US Army pilots who shot down at least one Japanese aircraft on December 7 stand in front of a P-36 fighter. From left to right: Lieutenant Lewis Sanders, Second Lieutenant Phillip Rasmussen, Second Lieutenant Ken Taylor, Lieutenant George Welch and Second Lieutenant Harry Brown. ✪

A damaged Japanese Zero fighter leaves a trail of smoke as it flies above Pearl Harbor. ✪

Bleary-eyed military personnel were still getting dressed as they rushed to their stations and took up battle positions.

Many of the planes parked at the army bases came under immediate and concentrated fire from Japanese Zero fighters which possessed both armour-piercing and incendiary bullets, the latter of which contained a phosphorous element causing fires to start.

Aircraft at the bases had been positioned in a close formation for security purposes and the surprise nature of the attack meant there was no time to move them. Lined up wingtip-to-wingtip, often in rows of more than 10, many of them were easy targets for the Japanese attack force.

Hangars and major barracks bore the brunt too, as infrastructure was targeted to ensure maximum long-term setbacks to US military development in the Pacific.

Some of the older facilities on Ford Island were constructed from wood and so burned quickly, fiercely and with plentiful smoke which created vision problems both for any airmen who did make it to their aircraft and for anti-aircraft gunners.

Despite a lack of preparedness or combat readiness, three Curtiss P-40 Kittyhawk pursuit aircraft which had been taking part in training exercises at Bellows Field successfully took off, but once airborne they were immediately downed by Japanese fighters. Several P-40s and Curtiss P-36 Mohawks from the Wheeler and Haleiwa bases managed to gain altitude and engage with their attackers, enjoying some success in shooting down Japanese planes whose pilots had not expected such as a rapid response after the success of their surprise offensive. Further Japanese aircraft were hit by a continuous barrage of US anti-aircraft fire, but their strength was overwhelming.

United States aircraft at Pearl Harbor

Hickam Field

Type	Number
Boeing B-17D Flying Fortress four-engine heavy bomber, 1939	12
Douglas A-20A Havoc two-engine attack/light bomber, 1940	13
Douglas B-18 Bolo two-engine standard bomber, 1936	33
Douglas C-33 (DC-2) two-engine freighter	2

Wheeler Field

Type	Number
Boeing P-26A Peashooter open cockpit pursuit, 1934	6
Boeing P-26B Peashooter open cockpit pursuit, 1935	6
Curtiss P-36A Mohawk pursuit, 1937	39
Curtiss P-40B Tomahawk pursuit, 1940	87
Curtiss P-40C Kittyhawk pursuit, 1941	11
Douglas BT-2 biplane, basic trainer	3
Grumman OAF-9 Goose observation amphibian	3
Martin B-12 two-engine medium bomber, 1934	3
North American AT-6 Texan, advanced trainer	2
Seversky AT-12A Guardsman, advanced trainer	1

Bellows Field

Type	Number
North American O-47B observation plane	6
Stinson O-49 Vigilant L-1 observation plane	2

Haleiwa Air Field

Type	Number
Curtiss P-36 Mohawk pursuit	2
Curtiss P-40 Kittyhawk pursuit	8

Naval Air Station Ford Island

Type	Number
Brewster F2A-3 Buffalo fighter, 1939	8
Consolidated PBY-1 Catalina patrol bomber, flying boat, 1936	2
Consolidated PBY-3 Catalina scout bomber, flying boat, 1937	15
Consolidated PBY-5 Catalina scout bomber, flying boat, amphibian, 1939	18
Douglas SBD-2 Dauntless scout/dive-bomber, 1941	3
Grumman F4F-3 Wildcat fighter, 1940	5
Grumman F4F-3A Wildcat fighter, 1941	5
Grumman J2F Duck single engine utility amphibian	19
Sikorsky JRS 18 passenger amphibian flying boat	9

Ewa Marine Corps Air Station

Type	Number
Douglas R3D-2 (DC-5) two-engine paratroop transport	2
Douglas SBD-1 Dauntless scout/dive-bomber, 1940	20
Douglas SBD-2 Dauntless scout/dive-bomber, 1941	3
Grumman F4F-3 Wildcat fighter	11
Grumman J2F-4 Duck utility floatplane, amphibian	2
Lockheed JO-2 Electra Junior, six seat transport	1
North American SNJ-3 Texan advanced trainer	1
Sikorsky JRS-1 Twin-engine, 18 passage flying boat	1
Vought SB2U-3 Vindicator scout/bomber	8

Naval Air Station Kaneohe

Type	Number
Consolidated PBY-5 Catalina patrol bomber, flying boat, amphibian, 1939	36
Vought OS2U Kingfisher amphibian	1

Smoke pours from P-40 fighters and aircraft hangars which have been destroyed at Wheeler Field. The way the smoke rises from the area shows how the planes were tightly positioned at the bases. ✪

Lieutenant George Welch, left, and Second Lieutenant Ken Taylor, right, pose for a photograph at Wheeler Field in January 1942 after they were each presented with the Distinguished Service Cross for their actions during the Pearl Harbor attack. ✪

A photograph taken at 5pm on December 7 shows bomb damage done to hangars at Hickam Field. ✪

Damaged cars and hangar building at Naval Air Station Kaneohe. ✪

A destroyed US fighter at Wheeler Field. ✪

George Welch and Ken Taylor

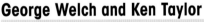

Among the pilots who took off to combat the Japanese were Second Lieutenant George Welch and his wingman Lieutenant Ken Taylor, both of the Army Air Corps. On the night prior to the Pearl Harbor attack, the pair had attended a formal Christmas dinner-dance event at a hotel in Waikiki and – not unusual for them – it had led to an all-night poker game.

As they returned to their barracks shortly before sunrise on December 7 still wearing their tuxedo trousers from the night before, the bombs began to drop. Welch and Taylor had both recently had their fighter planes moved to Haleiwa and while Taylor got his Buick, Welch telephoned the airstrip and demanded that two P-40s be readied.

Acting entirely on their own initiatives, they drove to the airfield – encountering enemy fire along the way – before taking off in their fuelled and armed Kittyhawks. Despite only having ammunition in their wing-mounted .30 calibre guns, the two of them recorded four confirmed kills along

with several probable shootings; in fact the two pilots accounted for 20% of all Japanese aircraft losses sustained during the attack.

Both men were nominated for America's top military award – the Medal of Honor – but because they had acted without direct orders these were downgraded to Distinguished Service Cross citations. However, the record of Welch's award contains far greater detail than any of the 15 Medal of Honour citations which were awarded for actions on December 7.

Rafe McCawley and Danny Walker, the main male characters in the 2001 blockbuster Hollywood film on Pearl Habor from director Michael Bay, are loosely based on Welch and Taylor.

Much artistic licence has been applied to their back stories but their actions – Rafe and Danny do manage to get airborne in two P-40s before they shoot down seven Japanese Zeros – are based on these real events. Taylor was less than complimentary of the cinema release, describing it as "over-sensationalised".

A destroyed SB2U Vindicator aircraft in flames at the Ewa Marine Corps base. ✪

A Japanese dive bomber is shot down. ✪

Text from the DSC citation for Second Lieutenant George S Welch

George S Welch
Second Lieutenant , 47th Pursuit Squadron, 15th Pursuit Group, Air Corps, United States Army

For extraordinary heroism in action over the Island of Oahu, Territory of Hawaii, and waters adjacent thereto, December 7, 1941:

When surprised by a heavy air attack by Japanese Forces on Wheeler Field and vicinity at approximately 8am, he left Wheeler Field and proceeded by automobile, under fire, to Haleiwa Landing Field, a distance of approximately 10 miles, where the planes of his squadron were stationed.

He immediately, on his own initiative, took off for the purpose of attacking the invading Japanese aircraft in attacking force, and proceeded to his initial point over Barbers Point. At time of take-off he was armed only with calibre .30 machine guns. Upon arrival over Barbers Point he observed a formation of approximately 12 planes over Ewa, about 1000ft below and 10 miles away. Accompanied only by one other pursuit ship, he immediately attacked this enemy formation and shot down an enemy dive bomber with one burst from three caliber .30 guns. At this point he discovered that one caliber .30 gun was jammed. While engaged in combat his plane was hit by an incendiary bullet, which passed through the baggage compartment just in the rear of his seat.

He climbed above the clouds, checked his plane, returned to the attack over Barbers Point, and immediately attacked a Japanese plane running out to sea, which he shot down, the plane falling into the ocean. No more enemy planes being in sight he proceeded to Wheeler Field to refuel and replenish ammunition. Just as refueling and reloading were completed but before his guns had been repaired, a second wave of about 15 enemy planes approached low over Wheeler Field. Three came at him and he immediately took off, headed straight into the attack, and went to the assistance of a brother officer, who was being attacked from the rear.

This enemy plane burst into flames and crashed about half way between Wahiawa and Haleiwa. During this combat his plane was struck by three bullets from the rear gun of the ship he was attacking. One striking his motor, one the propeller and one the cowling. This attack wave having disappeared, he returned to the vicinity of Ewa and found one enemy plane proceeding seaward, which he pursued and shot down about five miles off shore, immediately thereafter returning to his station at Haleiwa Landing Field.

Lieutenant Welch's initiative, presence of mind, coolness under fire against overwhelming odds in his first battle, expert maneuvering of his plane, and determined action contributed to a large extent toward driving off this sudden unexpected enemy air attack.

Air station personnel move a damaged Catalina away from burning hangars at Kaneohe. ✪

PBY Catalinas and US bombers

As would be proved by its eventual decisive defeat, Japan had reason to fear America's military might. However, one of the reasons Roosevelt had not fought against isolationism in government even harder was that he knew the forces at his disposal in

As black smoke rises from burning battleships in the background, photographers record damage done to the Ford Island seaplane ramp. ✪

1941 – although considerable and powerful – were not quite at a state of readiness for conflict, especially if it became conflict on two fronts.

Two unfolding events on the day of the Pearl Harbor attack would demonstrate this,

and they show how deficiencies in resources and tactical planning allowed such a surprise offensive to occur.

The first of these was the Japanese strafing of the Consolidated PBY Catalina aircraft at Kaneohe during the first wave, and by the end of the attack 33 of these had been destroyed. Dive-bombers obliterated 26 of the aircraft type on Ford Island, also. As the Catalinas were predominantly used for patrol, questions were soon asked as to why so many were idle on the day.

The answer, it seemed, was that parts were hard to come by, the navy lacked enough qualified airmen to pilot them and navy leaders were reluctant to overuse them before they were actually in a state of war, knowing they would be crucial to defending its fleet once conflict had begun.

As a result, few PBYs were used for patrol before December 7, and, crucially, most that did undertake operations were sent south toward the nearest Japanese territories which was the opposite direction to that from which the Pearl Harbor strike force had approached.

Compounding matters, the ineffectiveness of the US bomber group at Pearl Harbor became clear in the wake of the attack with the army possessing only 12 B-17 Flying Fortresses which were capable of long-range flight and patrol assignments.

With both still smouldering, destroyed PBY Catalina aircraft lie in front of a ruined hangar on Ford Island. ✪

A PBY patrol bomber in flames at Kaneohe. ✪

Smoke rises behind a US Army B-17 which managed to safely land at Hickam Field despite arriving unarmed during the Pearl Harbor attack. ✪

The B-17 bomber of First Lieutenant Karl T Barthelmess arrives at Pearl Harbor to find Japanese bombers flying overhead. ✪

Earlier in 1941, operations officers from both the US Navy and Army requested more patrol aircraft, citing Hawaii's susceptibility to attack without them but the resulting aircraft were diverted to England and the Philippines instead. It left them incapable of using patrols to repel an enemy aircraft carrier offensive.

Along with the 12 B-17s at Hickam were obsolete twin-engine B-18s which had limited range, armour and weapons capacity. On the morning of the Japanese attack, 16 B-17s were scheduled to land at Pearl Harbor for refuelling on their way to the Philippines. Twelve of them attempted to land during the attack and were fired upon by Japanese aircraft. Having originated in California more than 2000 miles away, to reduce weight the bombers made the trip without machine guns and so had no defence.

All managed to touch down – including an emergency landing on a nearby golf course, but a flare ignited in one B-17's radio compartment as it approached Hickam Field and it was gutted by the resulting fire making it the first American manned B-17 destroyed in the Second World War.

As yet more evidence of military unpreparedness, a B-24 Liberator was at Pearl Harbor to undergo work on its weapons capabilities and to have photography equipment fitted. Due to trouble fitting the machine guns, the job was delayed until Monday, December 8, and it was a sitting target for the Japanese bomb which destroyed it.

The shattered wreckage of bombed American planes strewn across Hickam Field. *Courtesy, PA*

Objectives achieved

Despite the valiant actions of the handful of US pilots credited with downing Japanese aircraft, there can be little doubt that the plan to neutralise American air forces at Pearl Harbor – both on the day of the attack and for the short-term future – was a comprehensive success.

Records of exactly how many aircraft were lost for both the US Army and Navy vary and depend on which counts are taken. What can be taken as certain is that more than 150 planes were destroyed and the same number again suffered significant damage – the total affected being more than three-quarters of the total forces based at Pearl Harbor's various facilities. The human toll was devastating also, with the Army Air Corps reporting 163 personnel killed, 43 missing and 336 wounded.

The damage done meant Japan controlled the airspace above Pearl Harbor and this allowed its comparatively slower and more laboured Kate bombers free rein to target the ships of the Pacific Fleet.

A US Marine Corps aircraft burns in the fields of Pearl Harbor. ✪

The wreckage of a B-17 bomber at Hickam Field is stark evidence of the damage Japan inflicted on US Army and Navy air forces during the Pearl Harbor attack. ✪

CHAPTER 10

THE PACIFIC FLEET AT PEARL HARBOR

The naval forces in Hawaii

The following list details the composition of the United States Pacific Fleet on the day of the Pearl Harbor attack. The individuals named are the commanding officers and the locations given indicate where the vessel was at the time...

Order of the United States Navy, December 7, 1941

Secretary of the Navy:
Secretary Frank Knox
Washington, DC

US PACIFIC FLEET

US Pacific Fleet
Admiral H E Kimmel
HQ at Pearl Harbor, Hawaii

BATTLE FORCE PACIFIC FLEET

Vice Admiral W S Pye

BATTLESHIPS, BATTLE FORCE

BATTLESHIP DIVISION 1
Rear Admiral I C Kidd
- USS *Nevada*, BB-36, Captain F W Scanland, Pearl Harbor
- USS *Pennsylvania*, BB-38, Captain C M Cooke Jr, Pearl Harbor, in dry dock
- USS *Arizona*, BB-39 (flagship), Captain F V Valkenburgh, Pearl Harbor

Observation Squadron 1
Lieutenant Commander W D Rowley

BATTLESHIP DIVISION 2
Rear Admiral D W Bagley
- USS *Oklahoma*, BB-37, Captain E J Joy, Pearl Harbor
- USS *Tennessee*, BB-43 (flagship), Captain C E Reordan, Pearl Harbor
- USS *California*, BB-44, Captain J W Bunkley, Pearl Harbor

Observation Squadron 2
Lieutenant Commander C W Haman

BATTLESHIP DIVISION 4
Rear Admiral W S Anderson
- USS *Colorado*, BB-45, Captain L E Lindsay, Bremerton, Washington, being overhauled
- USS *Maryland*, BB-46, Captain E W McKee, Pearl Harbor
- USS *West Virginia*, BB-48 (flagship), Captain M S Bennion, Pearl Harbor

Observation Squadron 4
Lieutenant Commander R G Lockhart

AIRCRAFT, BATTLE FORCE

CARRIER DIVISION 1
Rear Admiral A W Fitch
- USS *Lexington*, CV-2 (flagship), Captain F C Sherman, at sea, en route to Midway Island
- USS *Saratoga*, CV-3, Captain A H Douglas, San Diego, California, picking up her air group which had been training ashore

USS *Lexington* Air Group
Lieutenant Commander W B Ault
- Fighting Squadron 2
- Bombing Squadron 2
- Scouting Squadron 2
- Torpedo Squadron 2
- Utility Unit

USS *Saratoga* Air Group
Lieutenant Commander E A Cruise
- Fighting Squadron 3
- Bombing Squadron 3
- Scouting Squadron 3
- Torpedo Squadron 3
- Utility Unit

CARRIER DIVISON 2
Vice Admiral W F Halsey
- USS *Enterprise*, CV-6 (flagship), Captain G D Murray, at sea, en route from Wake Island

USS *Enterprise* Air Group
Lieutenant Commander H J Young
- Fighting Squadron 6
- Bombing Squadron 6
- Scouting Squadron 6
- Torpedo Squadron 6
- Utility Unit

Aircraft, Battle Force Pool
Fleet Air Photo Unit, Pacific
Advanced Carrier Training Group, Pacific

CRUISERS, BATTLE FORCE

CRUISER DIVISION 3
Rear Admiral A T Bidwell
- USS *Richmond*, CL-9, Captain A D Struble, at sea, en route to Valpariso, Chile
- USS *Concord*, CL-10 (flagship), Captain I C Sowell, San Diego, California, being overhauled
- USS *Trenton*, CL-11, Captain J H Brown Jr, Balboa, Panama Canal Zone

Cruiser Scouting Squadron 3
Lieutenant C C Howerton

CRUISER DIVISION 9
Rear Admiral H F Leary
- USS *Phoenix*, CL-46, Captain H E Fischer, Pearl Harbor
- USS *Boise*, CL-47, Captain S B Robinson, Pearl Harbor
- USS *Honolulu*, CL-48 (flagship), Captain H Dodd, Pearl Harbor, being overhauled
- USS *St Louis*, CL-49, Captain G A Rood, Pearl Harbor, being overhauled
- USS *Helena*, CL-50, Captain R H English, Pearl Harbor

Cruiser Scouting Squadron 9
Lieutenant Commander B C Lovett

DESTROYERS, BATTLE FORCE

DESTROYER FLOTILLA 1
Rear Admiral R A Theobald
- USS *Raleigh*, CL-7, Captain R B Simons, Pearl Harbor
- USS *Dobbins*, AD-3, Commander H E Paddock, Pearl Harbor
- USS *Whitney*, AD-4, Commander N M Pigman, Pearl Harbor

DESTROYER SQUADRON 1
Captain A R Early
- USS *Phelps*, DD-360, Commander W Nyquist, Pearl Harbor

Destroyer Division 1
Commander W S Popham
- USS *Dewey*, DD-349 (flagship), Commander A J Detzer Jr, Pearl Harbor, being overhauled
- USS *Hull*, DD-350, Lieutenant Commander R F Stout, Pearl Harbor
- USS *MacDonagh*, DD-351, Lieutenant Commander J M McIsaac, Pearl Harbor
- USS *Worden*, DD-352, Lieutenant Commander W G Pogue, Pearl Harbor

Destroyer Division 2
Commander C W Flynn
- USS *Farragut*, DD-348 (flagship), Lieutenant Commander G P Hunter, Pearl Harbor
- USS *Dale*, DD-352, Lieutenant Commander H E Parker, Pearl Harbor
- USS *Monaghan*, DD-354, Lieutenant Commander W P Burford, Pearl Harbor
- USS *Aylwin*, DD-355, Lieutenant Commander R H Rodgers, Pearl Harbor

DESTROYER SQUADRON 3
Commander T J Keliher
- USS *Clark*, DD-361, Commander M T Richardson, Mare Island, California, being overhauled

Destroyer Division 5
Commander L F Lovette
- USS *Reid*, DD-369, Lieutenant Commander H F Pullen, Pearl Harbor
- USS *Conyngham*, DD-371, Lieutenant Commander B S Anderson, Pearl Harbor
- USS *Cassin*, DD-371 (flagship) Lieutenant Commander D F J Shea, Pearl Harbor, in dry dock
- USS *Downes*, DD-375, Lieutenant Commander W R Thayer, Pearl Harbor, in dry dock

Destroyer Division 6
Commander A M Bledsoe
- USS *Cummings*, DD-365, Lieutenant Commander G D Cooper, Pearl Harbor
- USS *Case*, DD-370 (flagship), Lieutenant Commander R W Bedilion, Pearl Harbor
- USS *Shaw*, DD-373, Lieutenant Commander W G Jones, Pearl Harbor
- USS *Tucker*, DD-374, Lieutenant Commander W R Terrell, Pearl Harbor, in dry dock

DESTROYER SQUADRON 5
Captain H E Overesch
- USS *Porter*, DD-356, Lieutenant Commander F I Entwistle, at sea, escorting USS *Lexington*

Destroyer Division 9
Commander G C Kriner
- USS *Mahan*, DD-364, Lieutenant Commander R W Simpson, at sea, escorting USS *Lexington*
- USS *Drayton*, DD-366 (flagship), Lieutenant Commander L Abercrombie, at sea, escorting USS *Lexington*
- USS *Lamson*, DD-367, Lieutenant Commander P V Mercer, at sea, escorting USS *Lexington*
- USS *Flusser*, DD-368, Lieutenant Commander G H Lyttle, at sea, escorting USS *Lexington*

Destroyer Division 10
Commander J V Murphy
- USS *Cushings*, DD-376 (flagship), Lieutenant Commander C Noble, Mare Island, California, being overhauled
- USS *Perkins*, DD-377, Lieutenant Commander T F Wellings, Mare Island, California, being overhauled
- USS *Smith*, DD-378, Lieutenant Commander F X McInerney, Mare Island, California
- USS *Preston*, DD-379, Lieutenant Commander T J O'Brien, San Diego, California

DESTROYER FLOTILLA 2
Rear Admiral M F Draemel
- USS *Detroit*, CL-8, Captain L J Wiltse, Pearl Harbor
- USS *Dixie*, AD-14, Captain J G Moyer, Mare Island, California

DESTROYER SQUADRON 4
Captain J H S Dessez
- USS *Selfridge*, DD-357, Commander W Craig, Pearl Harbor

Destroyer Division 7
Commander L B Austin
- USS *Bagley*, DD-386, Lieutenant Commander G A Sinclair, Pearl Harbor, in dry dock
- USS *Blue,* DD-387 (flagship), Lieutenant Commander H N Williams, Pearl Harbor
- USS *Helm*, DD-388, Lieutenant Commander C E Carroll, Pearl Harbor
- USS *Henley*, DD-391, Lieutenant Commander R H Smith, Pearl Harbor

Destroyer Division 8
Commander S B Brewster
- USS *Mugford*, DD-389 (flagship), Lieutenant Commander E W Young, Pearl Harbor
- USS *Ralph Talbot*, DD-390, Lieutenant Commander R Earle Jr, Pearl Harbor
- USS *Patterson,* DD-392, Lieutenant Commander F R Walker, Pearl Harbor
- USS *Jarvis*, DD-393, Lieutenant Commander J R Topper, Pearl Harbor

DESTROYER SQUADRON 6
Captain R L Conolly
- USS *Balch*, DD-363, Commander C J Rend, at sea, escorting USS *Enterprise*

Destroyer Division 11
Commander C P Cecil
- USS *Gridley*, DD-380, Lieutenant Commander E A Simmons, at sea, escorting USS *Enterprise*
- USS *Craven*, DD-382, Lieutenant Commander C F M S Quinby, at sea, escorting USS *Enterprise*
- USS *McCalla*, DD-400, Lieutenant Commander F Moosbrugger, at sea, escorting USS *Enterprise*
- USS Maury, DD-401 (flagship), Lieutenant Commander E D Snare, at sea, escorting *USS Enterprise*

Destroyer Division 12
Commander E P Sauer
- USS *Dunlap*, DD-384 (flagship), Lieutenant Commander V R Roane, at sea, escorting USS *Enterprise*

- USS *Fanning*, DD-385, Lieutenant Commander W R Cooke Jr, at sea, escorting USS *Enterprise*
- USS *Benham*, DD-397, Lieutenant Commander F Worthington, at sea, escorting USS *Enterprise*
- USS *Ellet*, DD-398, Lieutenant Commander F H Gardner, at sea, escorting USS *Enterprise*

DESTROYER DIVISION 50
Commander A D Burhans
- USS *Rathburne*, DD-113, Lieutenant Commander R B Nickerson, Mare Island, California
- USS *Talbot*, DD-114, Lieutenant E A McFall, San Diego, California
- USS *Waters*, DD-115, Lieutenant H J Armstrong Jr, San Diego, California
- USS *Dent*, DD-116, Lieutenant P H Tobelman, San Diego, California

MINECRAFT, BATTLE FORCE

MINE SQUADRON 1
Rear Admiral W R Furlong
- USS *Oglala*, CM-4, Commander E F Speight

Mine Division 1
Commander J F Crowe Jr
- USS *Tracy*, DM-19, Lieutenant Commander G R Phelan, Pearl Harbor, being overhauled
- USS *Preble*, DM-20, Lieutenant Commander C F Chillingworth, Pearl Harbor, being overhauled
- USS *Sicard*, DM-21, Lieutenant Commander W C Schultz, Pearl Harbor, being overhauled
- USS *Pruitt,* DM-22 (flagship), Lieutenant Commander H G Beecher Jr, Pearl Harbor, being overhauled

Mine Division 2
Commander R P Whitemarsh
- USS *Gamble*, DM-15, Lieutenant Commander D A Crandall, Pearl Harbor
- USS *Ramsay*, DM-16, Lieutenant Commander G L Sims, Pearl Harbor
- USS *Montgomery*, DM-17, Lieutenant Commander R A Guthrie, Pearl Harbor
- USS *Breese*, DM-18, Lieutenant Commander H F Stout, Pearl Harbor

MINE SQUADRON 2
Commander G F Hussey Jr
- USS *Hopkins*, DMS-13, Lieutenant Commander R W Clark, at sea, training with USS *Indianapolis*

Mine Division 4
Commander W H Hart
- USS *Zane*, DMS-14, Lieutenant Commander L M LeHardy, Pearl Harbor, being overhauled
- USS *Wasmuth*, DMS-15, Lieutenant Commander J L Wilfong, Pearl Harbor
- USS *Trever*, DMS-16, Lieutenant Commander J S Smith Jr, Pearl Harbor
- USS *Perry*, DMS-17 (flagship), Lieutenant Commander R E Elliot, Pearl Harbor

Mine Division 5
Commander S H Hurt
- USS *Chandler*, DMS-9, Lieutenant Commander H H Tiemroth, at sea, training with USS *Minneapolis*
- USS *Southard*, DMS-10 (flagship), Lieutenant Commander J B Cochran, at sea, training with USS *Indianapolis*
- USS *Hovey*, DMS-11, Lieutenant Commander J E Florance, at sea, training with USS *Minneapolis*
- USS *Long*, DMS-12, Lieutenant Commander W S Weeder, at sea, training with USS *Indianapolis*

Mine Division 6
Commander E D Gibb
- USS *Dorsey*, DMS-1 (flagship), Lieutenant Commander R Mackinnon, at sea, training with USS *Indianapolis*
- USS *Lamberton*, DMS-2, Lieutenant Commander W J O'Brien, at sea, training with USS *Minneapolis*
- USS *Boggs*, DMS-3, Lieutenant Commander D G Roberts, at sea, training with USS *Minneapolis*
- USS *Elliott*, DMS-4, Lieutenant Commander C D Reynolds, at sea, training with USS *Indianapolis*

SCOUTING FORCE PACIFIC FLEET

Vice Admiral W Brown

CRUISERS, SCOUTING FORCE

Rear Admiral E H Newton

CRUISER DIVISON 4
Rear Admiral E H Newton
- USS *Pensacola*, CA-24, Captain N Scott, at sea, en route to Manila Bay
- USS *Salt Lake City*, CA-25, Captain E H Zacharias, training at sea
- USS *Chicago*, CA-29 (flagship), Captain B H Bieri, at sea with USS *Lexington*
- USS *Indianapolis*, CA-35, Captain E W Hanson, training at sea

Cruiser Scouting Squadron 4
Lieutenant Commander G A McLean

CRUISER DIVISION 5
Rear Admiral R A Spruance
- USS *Northampton*, CA-26 (flagship), Captain W D Chandler Jr, training at sea
- USS *Chester*, CA-27, Captain T M Shock, training at sea
- USS *Louisville*, CA-28, Captain E B Nixon, at sea, en route to Manila Bay
- USS *Portland*, CA-33, Captain C E Van Hook, at sea with USS *Lexington*

Cruiser Scouting Squadron 5
Lieutenant E A Junghas

CRUISER DIVISION 6
Rear Admiral F J Fletcher
- USS *New Orleans*, CA-32, Captain H H Good, Pearl Harbor, being overhauled

- USS *Astoria*, CA-34 (flagship), Captain P B Haynes, at sea with USS *Lexington*
- USS *Minneapolis*, CA-36, Captain F J Lowry, training at sea
- USS *San Francisco*, CA-38, Captain D J Callaghan, Pearl Harbor, being overhauled

Cruiser Scouting Squadron 6
Lieutenant Commander M T Evans

AIRCRAFT, SCOUTING FORCE

Rear Admiral J S McCain Sr

Patrol Wing 1
Rear Admiral P L Bellinger
- Patrol Squadron 11, Naval Air Station Kaneohe
- Patrol Squadron 12. Naval Air Station Kaneohe
- Patrol Squadron 14, Naval Air Station Kaneohe
- USS *Wright*, AV-1, Commander C W Weiber, at sea, en route to Midway Island
- USS *Avocet*, AVP-4, Lieutenant J A Johnson Jr, Pearl Harbor
- USS *Hulbert*, AVD-6 (flagship), Lieutenant Commander J M Lane, Pearl Harbor
- USS *Ballard*, AVD-10, Commander J R Dudley, at sea, en route to Mare Island, California

Patrol Wing 2
Rear Admiral P L Bellinger
- Patrol Squadron 22, Naval Air Station Ford Island
- Patrol Squadron 23, Naval Air Station Ford Island
- Patrol Squadron 24, Naval Air Station Ford Island
- USS *Curtiss*, AV-4 (flagship), Commander S P Ginder, Pearl Harbor
- USS *Tangier*, AV-8, Commander C A F Sprague, Pearl Harbor
- USS *Swan*, AVP-7, Lieutenant F E Hall, Pearl Harbor
- USS *Casco*, AVP-12, Commander T S Combs, Puget Sound, Washington
- USS *Thornton*, AVD-11, Lieutenant Commander W F Kilne, Pearl Harbor
- USS *McFarland*, AVD-14, Lieutenant Commander J L Kane, at sea, anti-submarine training

Patrol Wing 4
Commander G Rowe
- Patrol Squadron 41, Sitka, Alaska
- Patrol Squadron 42, Naval Air Station Ford Island
- Patrol Squadron 43, Naval Air Station Ford Island
- Patrol Squadron 44, Naval Air Station Ford Island
- USS *Teal*, AVP-5, Lieutenant A S Major Jr, Seattle, Washington
- USS *Pelican*, AVP-6, Lieutenant Commander J C Alderman, Mare Island, California
- USS *Williamson*, AVD-2 (flagship), Lieutenant Commander F N Kivette, Bremerton, Washington, being overhauled

- USS *Gillis*, AVD-12, Lieutenant Commander J P Heath, Sitka, Alaska

Aircraft, Scouting Force Pool
Transition Training Group, Pacific
- Patrol Squadron 13, San Diego, California

SUBMARINES, SCOUTING FORCE

Rear Admiral T Withers Jr
- USS *Seagull*, AM-30, Lieutenant Commander D B Candler, Pearl Harbor

SUBMARINE SQUADRON 4
Captain F A Daubin
- USS *Litchfield*, DD-336, Lieutenant Commander F H Ball, at sea
- USS *Widgeon*, ASR-1, Lieutenant J A Flenniken, Pearl Harbor

Submarine Division 41
Commander F M O'Leary
- USS *S-18*, SS-123, Lieutenant W J Millican, San Diego, California
- USS *S-23*, SS-128, Lieutenant J R Pierce, San Diego, California
- USS *S-27*, SS-132, Lieutenant W S Stovall Jr, Mare Island, being overhauled
- USS *S-28*, SS-133, Lieutenant J D Crowley, Mare Island, California, being overhauled
- USS *S-34*, SS-139, Lieutenant T L Wogan, San Diego, California
- USS *S-35*, SS-140, Lieutenant J E Stevens, San Diego, California

Submarine Division 42
Commander C H Roper
- USS *Argonaut*, SS-166* (flagship), Lieutenant Commander S G Barchet, at sea, patrolling near Midway Island
- USS *Narwhal*, SS-167 (flagship), Lieutenant Commander C W Wilkins, Pearl Harbor
- USS *Nautilus*, SS-168, Lieutenant Commander J P Thew, Mare Island, California
- USS *Dolphin*, SS-169, Lieutenant Commander G B Rainer, Pearl Harbor
- USS *Cachalot*, SS-170, Lieutenant Commander W N Christensen, Pearl Harbor
- USS *Cuttlefish*, Lieutenant M P Hottel, Mare Island, California, being overhauled

Submarine Division 43
Commander N S Ives
- USS *Plunger*, SS-179 (flagship), Lieutenant D C White, at sea, en route to Pearl Harbor
- USS *Pollack*, SS-180, Lieutenant Commander S P Mosely, at sea, en route to Pearl Harbor
- USS *Pompano*, SS-181, Lieutenant Commander L S Parks, at sea, en route to Pearl Harbor

SUBMARINE SQUADRON 6
Captain A R McCann
- USS *Pelias*, AS-14, Commander W Wakefield, Pearl Harbor
- USS *Ortollan*, ASR-5, Lieutenant F D Latta, San Diego, California

Submarine Division 61
Commander C D Edmunds
- USS *Tambor*, SS-198 (flagship), Lieutenant Commander J W Murphy Jr, at sea, patrolling Wake Island
- USS *Tautog*, SS-199, Lieutenant Commander J H Willingham Jr, Pearl Harbor
- USS *Thresher*, SS-200, Lieutenant Commander W L Anderson, at sea, patrolling 50 miles north of Oahu
- USS *Triton*, SS-201, Lieutenant Commander W A Lent, at sea, patrolling Wake Island
- USS *Trout*, SS-202, Lieutenant Commander F W Fenno Jr, at sea, patrolling Midway Island
- USS *Tuna*, SS-203, Lieutenant Commander J J Crane, Mare Island California, being overhauled

Submarine Division 62
Commander F M O'Leary
- USS *Gar*, SS-206, Lieutenant Commander D McGregor, at sea, en route to California
- USS *Grayling*, SS-209, Lieutenant Commander E Olsen, at sea, en route to California
- USS *Gudgeon*, SS-211, Lieutenant Commander E W Grenfell, Maui, Hawaii

SUBMARINE SQUADRON 8
No commander assigned
- USS *Fulton*, AS-11, Commander A D Douglas, at sea, en route to Balboa, Panama Canal Zone
*never formally designated, but hull number was reserved

BASE FORCE PACIFIC FLEET

Rear Admiral W L Calhoun
- USS *Mercury*, AK-42, Lieutenant Commander G W Graber, Pearl Harbor
- USS *Aroostook*, AK-44, Puget Sound, Washington
- USS *Argonne*, AG-31, Commander F W Connor, Pearl Harbor
- USS *Sumner*, AG-32, Commander W B Coleman, Pearl Harbor
- USS *Ramapo*, AO-12, Commander D Curry Jr, Pearl Harbor
- USS *Sepulga*, AO-20, Commander A R Ponto, en route from San Pedro, California

SERVICE SQUADRON 2
Rear Admiral W L Calhoun
- USS *Sonoma*, AT-12, Lieutenant Commander J A Quellet, at sea, en route to Pearl Harbor
- USS *Sciota*, AT-30, Lieutenant W R Brown, Pearl Harbor
- USS *Pinola*, AT-33, Lieutenant A A Griese, San Pedro California
- USS *Keosanqua*, AT-38, Lieutenant Commander P M Boltz, Pearl Harbor
- USS *Navajo*, AT-64, Lieutenant Commander H B McLean, Pearl Harbor
- USS *Seminole*, AT-65, Lieutenant Commander W G Fewell, at sea, en route to San Diego, California

- USS *Solace*, AH-5, Captain B Perlman, Pearl Harbor
- USS *Medusa*, AR-1, Commander A E Schrader, Pearl Harbor
- USS *Vestal*, AR-4, Commander R P Luker, Pearl Harbor
- USS *Rigel*, AR-11, Captain R Dudley, Pearl Harbor, being overhauled
- USS *President Jackson*, AP-37, Commander C W Weitzel, not yet stationed at Pearl Harbor
- USS *President Adams*, AP-38, Commander C W Brewington, not yet stationed at Pearl Harbor
- USS *President Hayes*, AP-39, Commander F W Benson, New York Naval Yard
- USS *Crescent City*, AP-40, Commander W C Calhoun, Norfolk, Virginia

Fleet Post Office, Pearl Harbor
Fleet Motion Picture Exchange, Pearl Harbor

SERVICE SQUADRON 4
- USS *Henderson*, AP-1, Commander C F Martin, Pearl Harbor
- USS *Chaumont*, AP-5, Commander D R Tallman, at sea, en route to Manila Bay
- USS *William W Burrows*, AP-6, Commander R A Dierdorff, at sea, en route to Wake Island
- USS *Harris*, AP-8 (flagship), Captain O M Fosterr, San Diego, California
- USS *Zeilin*, AP-9, Captain P Buchanan, Seattle, Washington, being overhauled
- USS *Grant*, AP-29, Captain H R Hein, Pearl Harbor
- USS *St Mihiel*, AP-32, Commander E B Rogers, Pearl Harbor
- USS *Republic*, AP-33, Commander G Clark, at sea, en route to Manila Bay
- USS *Alchiba*, AK-23, Commander J S Freeman Sr, Pearl Harbor

SERVICE SQUADRON 6
Captain M C Bowman

Utility Wing 4
Commander J L Murphy
- Utility Squadron 1, Pearl Harbor
- Utility Squadron 2, Pearl Harbor and Naval Air Base Johnston Island
- Utility Squadron 3, Naval Air Base Puunene
- Aviation Repair Unit, Pearl Harbor

Aircraft, Service Force Pool

Mine Division 10**
- USS *Bobolink*, AM-20, Lieutenant J L Foley, Pearl Harbor
- USS *Grebe*, AM-43, Lieutenant Commander E D McEathron, Pearl Harbor
- USS *Kingfisher*, AM-25, Lieutenant Commander C B Schiano, Pearl Harbor
- USS *Vireo*, AM-52, Lieutenant Commander F J Ilsemann, Pearl Harbor

Mine Division 11**
- USS *Robin*, AM-3, Lieutenant D G Greenlee Jr, at sea, en route to Naval Air Base Johnston Island

- USS *Turkey*, AM-13, Lieutenant Commander T F Fowler, Pearl Harbor
- USS *Rail*, AM-26, Lieutenant Commander F W Beard, Pearl Harbor
- USS *Tern*, AM-31, Lieutenant W B Pendleton, Pearl Harbor

Anti-Aircraft Artillery School, Pearl Harbor
- USS *Utah*, AG-16

Fleet Machine Gun School
Fleet Camera Party
Target Repair Base
Mine Assembly Base
Mobile Degaussing Unit

SERVICE SQUADRON 8
Captain C H Maddox
- USS *Castor*, AKS-1, Commander H J Wright, Pearl Harbor
- USS *Antares*, AKS-3 (flagship), Commander L C Grannis, at sea, off Pearl Harbor
- USS *Bridge*, AF-1, Commander W B Jackson Jr, Mare Island, California
- USS *Artic*, AF-7, Commander C E Olsen, Maui, Hawaii
- USS *Boreas*, AF-9, Commander R K Davis, San Francisco, California
- USS *Aldebaran*, AF-10, Captain R W Abbott, San Francisco, California
- USS *Pyro*, AE-1, Commander N Vytlacil, Pearl Harbor
- USS *Lassen*, AE-3, Captain S Mills, Pearl Harbor
- USS *Kanawha*, AO-1, Commander K S Reed, Mare Island, California
- USS *Cuyama*, AO-3, Commander P R Coloney, San Diego, California
- USS *Brazos*, AO-4, Commander T J Kelly, at sea, en route to Dutch Harbor, Alaska
- USS *Neches*, AO-5, Commander W R Fletcher Jr, at sea, en route to Pearl Harbor
- USS *Tippicanoe*, AO-21, Commander A Macondray Jr, Wilmington, Califorina
- USS *Neosho*, AO-23, Commander J S Phillips, Pearl Harbor
- USS *Platte*, AO-24, Commander R H Henkle, Los Angeles, California
- USS *Sabine*, AO-25, Commander H L Maples, Mare Island, California
- USS *Kaskaskia*, AO-27, Commander W L Taylor, Mare Island, California, being overhauled

**these divisions may have formed after Pearl Harbor, but the eight minelayers were part of Service Squadron 6

AMPHIBIOUS FORCE PACIFIC FLEET

On December 7, 1941, the Amphibious Force consisted of the US Army's 3rd Infantry Division under army operation control, the 2nd Marine Division, the 2nd Marine Aircraft Wing, the 2nd Defense Battalion and depot.

CHAPTER 11

USS *Arizona*

Death of an American battleship

The destruction and sinking of USS *Arizona* remains the defining moment of the Pearl Harbor attack and a symbol of the devastation, resilience and recovery that occurred during and after the events of December 7, 1941...

As dive-bombers and fighters inflicted massive damage on US Army and Navy air forces, the 89 Nakajima B5N2 Kate aircraft which were part of the first wave launched attacks against the ships of the Pacific Fleet. With no US aircraft carriers in Pearl Harbor on December 7, the main targets were the eight battleships which were stationed there and among them was the USS *Arizona* which had been a prized asset of the expanding US Navy for more than 25 years.

A brief history

On March 16, 1914, the New York Navy Yard laid down the keel to begin construction of battleship 39 – later named the USS *Arizona*. The Pennsylvania-class vessel was a continuation of American naval policy to build one of the world's greatest seafaring forces and was part of a global naval arms race which saw both Great Britain and Japan – among others – dramatically increase their fleets.

The ship was launched on June 19, 1915, but construction continued on the floating hull until it was finally commissioned in October the year after. Problems with her engines meant it took until March of 1917 before work was finally complete and the *Arizona* was able to serve with the Atlantic Fleet during the First World War.

In the peaceful interwar years of the 1920s, *Arizona* was rarely called upon for anything more than training exercises but as the threat of conflict grew she was given a thorough modernisation – starting in 1929 – which saw the introduction of torpedo bulges, new armour for protection against air attack, new boilers, new turbines and new tripod masts. The work was completed by March 1931.

During the time before and after the overhaul, *Arizona* served as the flagship to several battleship divisions of the US Navy with operations taking place on both sides of the Atlantic.

In late 1940 she underwent further upgrades including additional anti-aircraft weaponry in preparation for exercises at Pearl Harbor's naval station.

A B5N2 bomber flying above Pearl Harbor with the burning *Arizona* in the background. ✪

The Atlantic Fleet battleships, with *Arizona* at the foreground, at sea in 1917. ✪

USS *Arizona* in the East River, New York, in mid-1916.

Looking south toward Ford Island, the smoke from *Arizona* pours westward back across the base presenting huge challenges to US anti-aircraft gunners. ✪

Destruction of the *Arizona*

Along with its fellow Battle Force vessels, USS *Arizona* was moored off Ford Island in Pearl Harbor on the morning Japan launched its attack. Almost instantly, the ships were targeted and the bombs began to rain down; a Kate from the *Kaga* carrier hitting Turret 4 causing minor damage and a small fire.

As the air raid sirens blasted through the ship, waking the crew from their slumbers, sailors on board fired the *Arizona's* anti-aircraft guns and it's believed they shot down two Japanese aircraft. They were instructed to go to Condition Z – or ZED – a full state of battle readiness.

The crew would not be given the chance to mount more significant opposition, however, as at 8.06am another B5N – this

one from *Hiryu* – hit the vessel between number one and two turrets on the starboard side with an armour-piercing 1700lb bomb which smashed through the decks and led to the detonation of the nearby forward magazine ammunition. The impact was fatal.

The forward part of the ship was completely gutted by the blast with the foremast and forward superstructure collapsing into the void which had been created. Turrets 1 and 2, now with no support, dropped more than 20ft from their normal positions and furious fires ripped through the vessel, ravaging the inside and producing vast plumes of thick black smoke visible for miles. It took a mere nine minutes for the *Arizona* to hit

the bottom of Pearl Harbor; the explosion, fires and subsequent sinking killing 1177 of the 1512 crewmen on board which is just a little less than half of the total number of lives lost on the day.

The shallow waters meant some of the superstructure was still exposed and the fire aboard the partially sunken *Arizona* continued to burn for two days.

On December 13, just five days after the attack, an official US Navy report on the 'Japanese Raid on Pearl Harbor' was produced and its Enclosure E provided the 'Action Report USS *Arizona* (BB39) December 7, 1941'.

In it, eight survivors who were aboard the ship that day gave statements on what they had witnessed.

The explosion of USS *Arizona's* forward magazine. ✪

STATEMENT

Ensign Jim D Miller,
US Navy

I had gotten up at about 0745, and had started to dress when a short air raid alarm sounded. The Arizona's air raid alarm consisted of the sounding of three blasts of a warning howler over the general announcing system. What I heard was only one short blast as though someone had accidentally touched the switch. I felt one explosion near the ship which seemed to me like a no-load shot on No 2 Catapult.

However it was followed by two more explosions, and I decided it was not a no-load shot, but of course had no idea just what the explosions were. Then the word was passed to set Condition ZED below the third deck. I slipped on a uniform and started to go down to the third deck to check up on the watertight doors and hatches.

I still did not realize that there was actually an air raid. As soon as I came up to the second deck from the lower wardroom, I met a gunner's mate who said he was trying to find the magazine keys. I went into the captain's cabin to call him and get the keys if possible. The captain was not there. I then looked in the gunnery officer's stateroom to see if I could get the keys from him, but he was not in either. By that time the gunner's mate had left me, and I went on down to the third deck.

General Quarters was sounded. I went into Turret 3 through the lower handling room to the booth, took the turret officer's station and manned the 2JE phones to Plot. Communications to Plot were OK. However, Turret 3 was the only turret I heard on the line. Shortly after I had reached the booth the turret was shaken by a bomb explosion of not very great intensity. After a minute or two a much more terrific explosion shook the turret. Smoke poured in through the overhang hatch, and I could see nothing but reddish flame outside.

The 2JE phones went dead, all power went off the turret, and all lights went out. From all reports that I could get from inside the turret, the turret was not even half manned. I believe that it was at about this time that a bomb hit on the starboard side of the quarterdeck next to Turret 4, penetrated down to the third deck and exploded. From later examination I found that this bomb had glanced off the side of Turret IV and then had penetrated the decks.

My lower handling room crew was shaken up, and water began coming into the lower handling room. Explosion gases were filling the turret from the overhang hatch and from openings into the lower room. I stepped outside the turret to see what the condition was on the quarterdeck. There were several small fires on the deck and awnings. I noticed several badly burned men lying on deck and saw Ensign Anderson, who had been Junior Officer of the Deck, lying on deck with a bad cut on his head.

I figured that with the turret not completely manned, with all power off, and with the turret full of suffocating gas we could do nothing toward repelling the attack. I sent the word into the turret for all hands to come outside and fight fires. All hands came out. Ensign Field and Ensign Flanagan were at their battle stations in the lower handling room. They were the last to come out of the turret and reported to me that everybody had gotten out and that all hatches in the turret had been closed behind them.

I found all fire hoses already connected to plugs on the quarterdeck, but there was no water on the fire mains. An attempt to call the centre engine room on the ship's service telephones was unsuccessful because the ship's service telephones were out of commission. It was also impossible to reach the engine room because of fire and smoke and gas. The first lieutenant was on the quarterdeck and in charge. About all we could do was to try to put out fires and drag some of the wounded men under the protection of the overhangs of the turrets. We put out several of the small fires – papers and awnings on deck – with buckets of water.

Fuel oil was coming up from some place on the port side and was catching on fire. The ship was down by the bow, and the quarterdeck began to become awash starting at the break of the deck at frame 88. The main and forecastle decks forward of frame 88 were ablaze. Oil on top of the water was feeding the fire. At one time the first lieutenant asked me if I had seen the captain or the admiral. I told him I had been in the captain's cabin and had not seen him.

He wanted me to go down into the cabin and check again. White, T A, BM2c, and myself went down into the cabin and looked around, felt in the captain's bed, but could find no trace of him. However, it was dark and smoke was bad, and it is possible that we could have missed him. Nevertheless, I am sure he was not there. We did not go into the admiral's cabin. We came back up to the quarterdeck.

Our boats, which were tied up to the quays and booms, were manned by some of the men who had swum to them from the side of the ship. One of the first boats which came alongside was a motor launch from the Solace with a medical rescue party. This boat took all our stretcher cases off the quarterdeck. Of these men the only ones that I recognized were Ensign Schubert, Ensign Anderson, Stephenson, H D Sea1/c, and a ship's cook, name unknown. Most of the men who were burned were unrecognisable. Shortly after the stretcher cases had been removed to the Solace motor launch, the first lieutenant ordered abandon ship. All of our guns had ceased firing, the main, forecastle, and boat

decks were burning; smoke obstructed a view of the foremast and the forward part of the ship. All officers' quarters aft were flooded and the quarterdeck forward was awash. Our life rafts were cut down and put into the water [and] all hands ordered to go over the side.

Men found the rafts difficult to paddle, and most of them crawled aboard motor launches or started swimming toward Ford Island. The first lieutenant, Ensign Field, and about half a dozen men and myself were the last to leave in one of our 50ft motor launches. We picked up quite a few more men who were swimming toward the island. We made the officers' landing at Ford Island, and all hands went ashore except the boat crew, Ensign Field, and the first lieutenant. The latter said that he was going back out and try to pick up any more men he could find.

I was told to remain in charge of the men on Ford Island. We went to the air raid shelter at the north-eastern corner of the island. All injured men were sent to the air station hospital as fast as possible. The rest remained in the air raid shelter until the raid was clear.

Still billowing smoke, a shot of the sinking *Arizona* is captured from either a vessel on the channel or perhaps from across the shore. ✪

STATEMENT

Ensign G S Flannigan,
US Navy Reserve

About 8 o'clock I heard the air raid siren. I was in the bunk room and everyone in the bunk room thought it was a joke to have an air raid on Sunday. Then I heard an explosion. I was undressed. I climbed into some khaki clothing and shoes. Then the general alarm bell went.

I made for my GQ [general quarters] station.

I don't remember any word passed over the speaker system. My station was the lower room of Turret 3. Just as the men and I go down the ladder leading to the passageway between the lower rooms of Turret 3 and 4 a bomb exploded. The lights went out. It seemed to be on the third deck, starboard side between Turrets 3 and 4. When that bomb hit, it made a whish with a gust of hot air and sparks flew. There followed a very nauseating gas and smoke immediately afterwards.

Before this time, condition ZED had been set in the lower room of Turret 3, and the men in the passage and I were unable to get

out of the passageway. I beat on the door for some minutes before someone inside the turret opened the door. We got all the men that we could find in the passageway into the lower room, and then dogged down the passageway door. We were unable to dog down the door of the port passageway between 3 and 4 because it had been sprung by an explosion. The air in the turret was fairly clear for a while, but finally gas or smoke starting coming in.

The men made quite a bit of confusion at first but they were very obedient when Ensign Field and I ordered them to keep quiet. About this time we got a flashlight and saw the turret

was very misty with smoke. Just after this, we heard hissing noise which was later discovered to be air leaking from holes in the forward transverse bulkhead of the lower room. Ensign Field tried to get central station on the ship's service phone, but the phones were out. We also tried the sound powered phones which were also out.

Conditions from smoke were getting worse and worse. It was then that we decided that we would have to leave the lower room. We sent men up the ladder to open the hatches to the electric deck, shell room and pits. The men had difficulty opening the first hatch. Men were

coughing badly when it was finally opened. We sent them up to the pits on the double.

There were two men and Ensign Field and I left in the lower room when water entered the lower room. It was about eight inches deep when Ensign Field and I finally left. We were the last two up. We climbed the ladder closing all the hatches behind us. I took charge of the men in the pits, and Ensign Field went out on deck to help Lt Cmdr Fuqua. We saw smoke entering the pits through the pointers and trainers telescope slots. I urged the men to take off their shirts, and we closed the openings with the clothes. After a short time, we got word from Ensign

Field to come out on deck.

When we got out on deck, the ship seemed to be ablaze from the boatdeck forward. We then unlashed the life raft on the starboard side of Turret 3, and threw it in the water. I sent the men aboard the raft and shoved it off. I was then called aft, and helped wounded men in the barge, leaving for Ford Island and helped men to the front of the air raid shelter and into trucks taking them to medical aid. By this time, the ship was ablaze from forward of Turret 3 to the bow. There were not boats to make another trip when I returned to the landing. I went into the air raid shelter.

STATEMENT

**Ensign D Hein,
US Navy**

I left the J O [junior officers'] Mess at General Quarters. As I went to the boat deck, I noticed that some of starboard AA guns were firing. I think they were the forward ones. Then I went up to the signal bridge. I looked around and saw that there was nothing that I could do. I saw the admiral on the signal bridge. Then I went up to the nav bridge. The only people up there were the captain, the quartermaster and myself. The quartermaster asked the captain if he wanted to go into the conning tower but the captain did not want to, making phone calls.

Suddenly the whole bridge shook like it was in an earthquake, flame came through the bridge windows which had been broken by gunfire. We three were trying to get out the port door at the after end of the bridge during all this shaking, but could not. We staggered to the starboard side and fell on the deck just forward of the wheel. Finally I raised my head and turned it and saw that the port door was open. I got up and ran to it, and ran down the port ladders, passing through flames and smoke.

Then I climbed half way down the signal bridge ladder and had to jump to the boat deck as it was bent way under. Then I climbed down a handrail to the galley deck. The flames and smoke on the boat deck and galley deck were decreasing in intensity; I believe they were powder flames. I walked aft and down the ladder to the port quarterdeck. Then I walked to the other side and down the officers' ladder to the barge. Just before all this shaking the quartermaster reported that a bomb had struck No 2 turret.

Arizona is engulfed by flames and smoke after the explosion which obliterated her front section. *Courtesy, PA*

STATEMENT

Ensign W J Bush,
US Navy

At about two or three minutes before 0800 Sunday, I was asleep in my room when I faintly heard a siren. Shortly thereafter I distinctly heard GQ. I put some clothes on and went up from lower wardroom country to the second deck. Lt C T Janz was sending everyone in the vicinity to shelter below the armoured deck. I went down with Lt Janz and about 40 enlisted men. Before we could close the hatch, there were three violent blasts with flame and powder

fumes entering the compartment. I then told all personnel in the vicinity to get out and go topside to avoid the gas.

About 20 enlisted personnel and myself went topside. I saw the entire ship forward of No 3 turret to be a raging fire. I asked Ensign Davison about fighting the fire and he told me there was no water in the fire main. Shortly thereafter, Ensign Davison and myself got three boats clear of the oil fire on the water and

picked up the men in the water who had jumped to get clear of the fire. We took several boatloads of badly burned and injured men to Ford Island landing and continued picking up men in the water between the ship and the shore.

I took one boat alongside the quarter of the Arizona and waited until everyone gathered on the stern had been taken off. Ensign Lenning, Ensign Miller and Lt Cmdr Fuqua made sure no one else could be rescued from the after end of the ship before they left. We then picked the men up out of the water and put everyone ashore at Ford Island landing. Lt Cmdr Fuqua took one boat and left to search the water for injured men. After sending all injured men to the dispensary, we took the remainder to the air raid shelter below Admiral Bellinger's quarters. Ensign Davison assisted me in directing the rescue work even though he was badly burned himself.

The foremasts of the *Arizona* topple over into the gaping hole which the huge explosion has created in the forward part of the ship. *Courtesy, PA*

STATEMENT

**Ensign AR Schubert,
US Navy**

At about 0755 Sunday, December 7, I was shaving in the wardroom head of the USS Arizona. I heard the air raid siren sound over the announcing system for about one second's duration, followed by the passed word, "air raid". At the same time I could hear scattered gunfire. I went to my room and looked out the port, where I saw several low-winged monoplanes at low altitude flying away from the line of moored battleships, apparently having finished a bombing or torpedo attack. I then heard the general alarm sound and the word passed for general quarters, and put on a pair of dungarees and slippers to go to my general quarters station, secondary Conn.

There were during this time one or more explosions which filled the air with fumes and vented out the port. The worst explosion filled the inboard end of the room with flame and left a residue of orange smoke which continued to vent out the port. By this time the ship was down by the bow and sinking so rapidly that the lines from the ship to the after key were snapping. I took a breath of air from out the port and went into the passageway, aft and up through a stores hatch which had been blown open.

Lt Cmdr Fuqua was directing operations on the quarter deck. I assisted in opening the hatches and in getting the wounded, chiefly burn cases, into the launches sent from the USS Solace. The ship was still sinking rapidly and oil was burning on the water and spreading aft. Because of the damage received there was no pressure on the firemain with which to fight the fire.

I left the ship in the gig and returned in a motor boat with which we make two trips to the Ford Island landing removing men from the ship.

We picked up Ensign Lennig, USNR from the water, and I had the boat crew leave me off at the USS Solace to have a cut on my head and burns on my hand and arm dressed.

An incredibly rare colour image from the Pearl Harbor attack captures the moment the forward magazine of the *Arizona* exploded. The photograph is a still taken from a film which was being shot at the location. ✪

STATEMENT

Ensign H D Davison,
US Navy

It was just before colours, in fact, I had already sent the messenger down to make the 8 o'clock reports to the captain. Then I heard a dive bomber attack from overhead. I looked through my spyglass and saw the red dots on the wings. That made me wonder, but I still couldn't believe it until I saw some bombs falling. The first one hit up by the air station. I sounded the air raid alarm and notified the captain.

The captain and Lt Cmdr Fuqua came on deck, and the captain went on up to the bridge. Mr Fuqua told me to sound General Quarters. About that time we took a bomb hit on the starboard side of the quarterdeck, just about abreast of No 4 turret. We grabbed the men available and started dropping the deck hatches and leading out hoses on the quarterdeck.

About this time, the planes that had made the initial dive bomb attack strafed the ship. Mr Fuqua and I told all hands to get in the marine compartment. It was reported to us that we had a bomb in the executive officers' office. Mr Fuqua told me to call the centre engine room and get pressure on the fire mains. Then he went up to the boat deck. I told the boatswain's mate of the watch to do that. Then I went into the OD's booth to do it myself.

Just after I stepped in the booth we took another hit which seemed to be on the starboard side of the quarterdeck just about frame 88. The boatswain's mate and I were trapped in the booth by the flames. We started out of the booth, trying to run through the flames aft on the quarterdeck. We couldn't get through so we went over the lifeline into the water. I was conscious of a sweetish, sickening smell to the flame. After I got in the water, my first intention was to go to the key and then onto the quarterdeck or swim to the gangway and get aboard. But after I took one look at the ship, I decided that it was useless, she had settled down by the bow, and appeared broken in two. The foremast was toppled over; she was a mass of flames from the forecastle to just forward of Turret 3.

I was helped into a motor launch by Ensign Bush and another man. Then we in turn took the motor launch and picked up as many survivors as we could find in the water. We took them over to the landing at Ford Island. There we were met by Air Station Marines, who helped us get the wounded ashore.

After we had unloaded the motor launch Ensign Bush and I took the barge, which had come up and took it back over alongside the quarterdeck where we gathered another load of injured. On our return to Ford Island, we noticed three more boats alongside the Arizona, so we proceeded to the air raid shelter. Then I went up to the dispensary for first aid treatment.

An image taken from closer to the battleship shows the devastation wreaked on *Arizona* by the Japanese attack. *Courtesy, PA*

STATEMENT

Lieutenant Commander S G Fuqua, US Navy

I was in the ward room eating breakfast about 0755 when a short signal on the ship's air raid alarm was made. I immediately went to the phone and called the officer of the deck to sound general quarters and then shortly thereafter ran up to the starboard side of the quarter deck to see if he had received word. On coming out of the ward room hatch on the port side, I saw a Japanese plane go by, the machine guns firing, at an altitude of about 100ft.

As I was running forward on the starboard side of the quarter deck, approximately by the starboard gangway, I was apparently knocked out by the blast of a bomb, which I learned later had struck the face plate of No 4 turret on the starboard side and had glanced off and gone through the deck just forward on the captain's hatch, penetrating the decks and exploding on the third deck. When I came to and got up off the deck the ship was a mass of flames amidships on the boat deck and the deck aft was awash to about frame 90. The anti-aircraft battery and machine guns apparently were still firing at this time. Some of the Arizona boats had pulled clear of the oil and were lying off the stern.

At this time I attempted, with the assistance of the crews of No 3 and No 4 turrets to put out the fire which was coming from the boat deck, and which had extended to the quarter deck. There was no water on the fire mains. However, about 14 CO2's were obtained that were stowed on the port side and held the flames back from the quarter deck in order to pick up wounded who were running down the boat deck out of the flames.

I placed about 70 wounded and injured in the boats, which had been picked up off the deck aft and landed them at the Ford Island landing. This was completed about 0900 or 0930. Not knowing whether the captain or the admiral had ever reached the bridge, I had the captain's hatch opened up, immediately after I came to, and sent officers Ensign G B Lenning, USNR and Ensign J D Miller, USN down to search the captain's and admiral's cabins to see if they were there. By that time the captain's cabin and admiral's cabin were about waist deep in water. A search of the two cabins revealed that the admiral and captain were not there. Knowing that they were on board I assumed that they had proceeded to the bridge. All personnel, but three or four men from turrets No. 3 and No. 4 were saved.

About 0900, seeing that all guns of the anti-aircraft and secondary battery were out of action and that the ship could not possibly be saved, I ordered all hands to abandon ship.

From information received from other personnel on board, a bomb had struck the forecastle, just about the time the air raid siren, at 0755. A short interval thereafter, there was a terrific explosion on the forecastle, apparently from the bomb penetrating the magazine. Approximately 30 seconds later a bomb hit the boat deck, apparently just forward of the stack and one went down the stack and one hit the face plate of No 4 turret. It is not known whether a torpedo hit the ship, but I have heard indirectly that the commanding officer of the USS Vestal stated that two torpedoes passed under his vessel which was secured alongside the Arizona, and struck the Arizona.

The first attack occurred about 0755. I saw approximately 15 torpedo planes, which had come in to the attack from the direction of the Navy Yard. These planes also strafed the ship after releasing their torpedoes. Shortly thereafter there was a dive-bomber and strafing attack of about 30 planes. This attack was very determined, planes diving within 500ft before releasing bombs. I believe there was a third attack of horizontal bombers about 0900, these planes came in from ahead at a height of about 10,000ft. There were about 12 planes in the flight that I saw.

The personnel of the anti-aircraft and machine gun batteries on the Arizona lived up to the best traditions of the Navy. I could hear guns firing on the ship long after the boat deck was a mass of flames. I cannot single out any one individual who stood out in acts of heroism above the others, as all of the personnel under my supervision conducted themselves with the greatest heroism and bravery.

From left to right are battleships USS *West Virginia*, USS *Tennessee* and the stricken USS *Arizona* which is almost completely obscured by thick black smoke. *Courtesy, PA*

STATEMENT

Chief Gunner's Mate J A Doherty, US Navy

I was in the chief's quarter when the air raid alarm sounded. At the same time I heard something hit. I went immediately to my battle station – which is the AA battery. When I arrived on the boat deck, I saw the forecastle waving up and down and fire and smoke coming up through seams of the deck.

I went to the port side to see if the ammunition hoists were rigged and they were okay. I then went to the starboard side and the crew was rigging No 1-3 hoist for hoisting ammunition. I noticed No 3 gun wasn't firing due to safety bearing when the foot firing mechanism cut out. I was then shocked and surrounded by smoke and flames. I was backing away from the smoke and I can't remember much from then on.

I was in the water and was helped in a boat and from there to a hospital. Only man dead and I'm not sure was Anderson, BM2c I think was hit by machine gun bullets.

This photograph, which was taken on February 2, 1942, shows the wreckage of the *Arizona* resting on the bottom of Pearl Harbor. *Courtesy, PA*

The damage to the foremast structure, bridge and Turret 2 show why *Arizona* was deemed a 'total loss' and no salvage operation was attempted. ✪

USS ARIZONA (BB39)   17 FEB., 1942
FOREMAST STRUCTURE, CONNING TOWER, AND TOP OF TURRET #2

Aftermath, salvage and memorial

In the days after the attack, several sailors received medals for their acts of bravery under fire including Lieutenant Commander Samuel G Fuqua – the ship's damage control officer – who earned the Medal of Honor for his efforts in tackling fires and helping injured survivors to shore. A posthumous Medal of Honor was given to Rear Admiral Isaac C Kidd, who became the first US flag officer to be killed in the Pacific war, and Captain Franklin Van Valkenburgh who was on the bridge attempting to defend the *Arizona* when the final bomb exploded the ammunition magazines and sunk her.

The battleship was declared temporarily out of service on December 29 and, while many of the vessels sunk during the attack were to be salvaged, repaired and relaunched, the damage done to the *Arizona* was so great that she would never be fit for service again. On December 1, 1942, she was removed from the Naval Vessel Register for good.

Later that year the surviving pieces of superstructure were scrapped and the main armaments were salvaged with gun turrets being installed as defences at US military locations in Hawaii. The guns from Turret 2 were later installed on the USS *Nevada* and were fired against the islands of Okinawa and Iwo Jima as the US Navy forced a Japanese surrender.

The remaining hull was left submerged as a wreck and both during and after the Second World War support began to grow for the idea of using the *Arizona* as a memorial to the victims of the Pearl Harbor attack and more generally to those who'd sacrificed their lives in the subsequent Pacific conflict.

In 1949, the Pacific War Memorial Commission was created with the purpose of erecting a permanent place of remembrance somewhere in Hawaii.

US Navy divers work around the *Arizona's* aft turrets. *Courtesy, PA*

An overview of the *Arizona* hull taken in the 1950s, prior to the construction of the memorial. ✿

USS VESTAL AR 4

A recent aerial view of the USS *Arizona* Memorial with a US Navy tour boat moored at the pier as visitors disembark to view the structure. ✪

USS ARIZONA BB 39

Known as the 'tears of the *Arizona*', oil, which is still escaping the wreck, is visible on the surface alongside one of the battleship's turret rings, above, and from the submerged structure, main. *Courtesy, James G Howes*

Admiral Arthur W Radford, commander of the Pacific Fleet, attached a flagpole to the *Arizona's* main mast in 1950 and began a tradition of hoisting and lowering the flag. He wished to extend this with the building of a temporary memorial but was denied the budget because of the ongoing Korean War, however in 1958 President Dwight D Eisenhower did finally approve the creation of a National Memorial.

Several different opinions existed as to what should be commemorated; some wanted it to be dedicated to just the crewmembers of the ship, others to all those who died in the Pacific theatre. As Congressional funding was required, the US government passed legislation which declared the *Arizona* would 'be maintained

in honour and commemoration of the members of the armed forces of the United States who gave their lives to their country during the attack on Pearl Harbor, Hawaii, on December 7, 1941'.

The USS *Arizona* Memorial was officially dedicated on May 30, 1962 – Memorial Day in America – and four years later was listed on the National Register of Historic Places.

Battleship USS *Missouri* – on the deck of which Japan officially offered its surrender during the Second World War – was moved to Pearl Harbor in 1999 and docked behind the *Arizona*; the pairing of the two meant to symbolise the beginning and end of US involvement in the conflict. Today, visitors to the memorial regularly top one

million annually and it's still the site of the traditional remembrance services.

As an active US cemetery, survivors of the *Arizona* from the day of the Pearl Harbor attack can have their ashes placed within the structure of the ship, while previous crew members can have their remains scattered in the waters above.

Of the many myths which exist around Pearl Harbor, the belief that the *Arizona* is – like the USS *Constitution* – perpetually in commission is one of the most common. The vessel actually now comes under the jurisdiction of the American National Park Service, although the navy retains the title and the *Arizona* is permitted to fly the Star Spangled Banner as if she were still a commissioned ship.

CHAPTER 12

BATTLESHIP ROW

America's capital ships are hit in two waves

With the USS *Arizona* burning, Japan's aircraft continued to swarm over Pearl Harbor, launching ferocious assaults on their targets. The damage done during both the first and second waves would impact on each of eight battleships in Hawaii at the time, along with many other vessels of the Pacific Fleet...

The massive explosion which rocked the *Arizona* had been caused by a converted naval shell carried by 49 of the Kate level bombers which comprised the first wave. They were Type 91 Model 5 bombs which weighed 1763lb; when dropped from altitude their streamlined design meant they impacted with tremendous force and could penetrate several decks before exploding. The Type 91 was responsible for the sinking of the *Arizona*, but only that capital ship would be sunk by one of these bombs. The rest would fall victim to a different weapon.

Kate bombers launch torpedo attacks

As Japanese Vals and Zeros bombed and strafed the various air force installations of Pearl Harbor, B5N2 Kates were dropping their payloads to target Battleship Row. In the first wave, 40 of the aircraft carried the Type 91 Model 2 torpedo boasting a 452lb warhead which exploded below the water line doing incredible damage.

The weapon had been upgraded specifically for the Pearl Harbor attack too, with the addition of wooden tail fins which kept the torpedo from sinking into the mud in shallow waters; exactly the conditions it

Japanese Zeros can be seen flying overhead as a bomb or torpedo detonates in the waters near Battleship Row. It would appear that this particular weapon missed its intended target. ✪

would encounter on December 7. It was the fins, pioneered by the British in their attack on the Italian fleet a year earlier, which distinguished the Type 91 Model 2 from the original Type 91. The bombs did significant damage, but the torpedoes were deadly, and accounted for damage to five of the seven

ships moored at Ford Island and several other sinkings across Pearl Harbor.

In the second wave, the Val dive-bombers switched roles with the Kates. As oil and fuel fires breathed huge plumes of smoke across Battleship Row the Kates were unable to target the vessels with any accuracy and so it was left to the faster D3As which were capable of passing their targets at high speeds and heights of just a few hundred feet.

Unable to carry torpedoes and holding significantly lighter bombs, the Vals inflicted far less damage on the ships than the Kates – but that's also down to the fact that the first wave had been so effective at crippling Battleship Row.

However the Vals did have success in attacking the dry dock where the battleship USS *Pennsylvania* was undergoing work, and in chasing down and effectively grounding the USS *Nevada* which managed to get under way.

A Kate bomber stalks Pearl Harbor. ✪

BATTLESHIP ROW ON DECEMBER 7, 1941

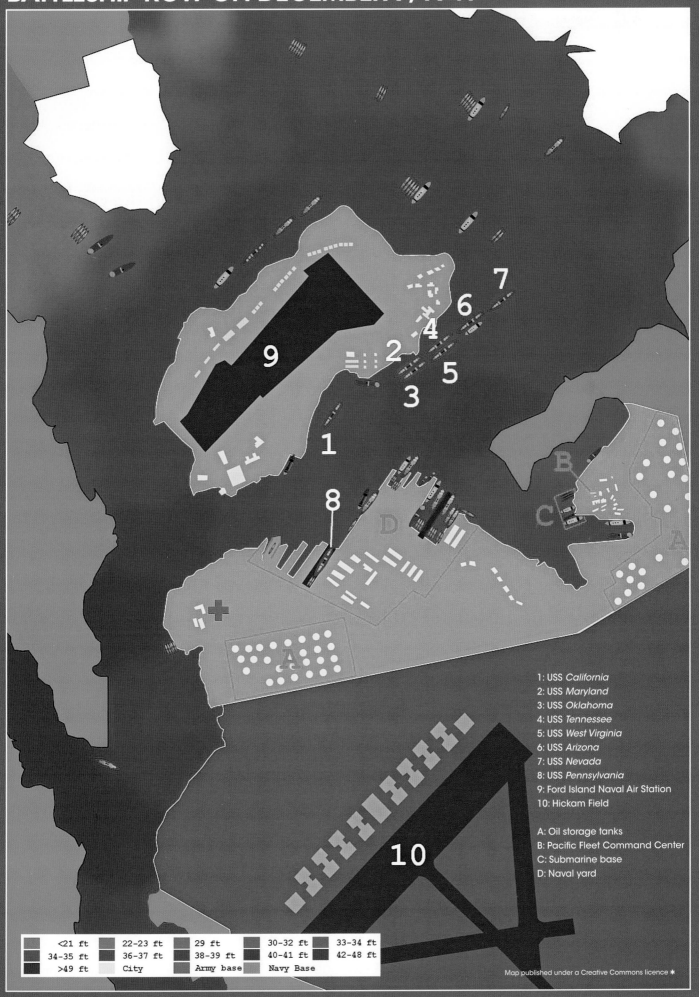

1: USS *California*
2: USS *Maryland*
3: USS *Oklahoma*
4: USS *Tennessee*
5: USS *West Virginia*
6: USS *Arizona*
7: USS *Nevada*
8: USS *Pennsylvania*
9: Ford Island Naval Air Station
10: Hickam Field

A: Oil storage tanks
B: Pacific Fleet Command Center
C: Submarine base
D: Naval yard

<21 ft	22–23 ft	29 ft	30–32 ft	33–34 ft
34–35 ft	36–37 ft	38–39 ft	40–41 ft	42–48 ft
>49 ft	City	Army base	Navy Base	

THE ATTACK BEGINS

A photo taken from a Japanese aircraft shows smoke rising from the airfields of Pearl Harbor as the torpedoes and bombs start to drop on Battleship Row. Ripples in the water suggest that payloads are either on their way or may have just impacted, and what looks like an oil slick coming from USS *West Virginia* indicates that she might already have been hit. For the next hour-and-a-half these seven vessels would come under continuous and fierce attack from bombers and dive-bombers of the Imperial Japanese Navy, and within just a few short minutes of this image being taken the skies around would be cast under the shadow of thick black smoke billowing from mangled wrecks of metal, fuel and oil. ✪

BATTLESHIP ROW

3: USS *Oklahoma*
Nevada-class battleship
BB-37

OUTCOME

Being positioned outboard of USS *Maryland*, *Oklahoma* bore the brunt of Japanese torpedo attacks and was hit by several on her port side. The ship was ripped open and as water poured in she rolled over and sank to the bottom of the harbour. Many of the men trapped in her upturned hull were cut free, but the sinking still resulted in the loss of more than 400 crewmen.
In 1943, *Oklahoma* was salvaged, patched up and refloated, but she was deemed too old and damaged to return to service and was formally decommissioned. On her way to be scrapped after the Second World War, *Oklahoma* sank while under tow from Hawaii to California.

CREW LOST: 429

0750 |

The crew of *Oklahoma* first become aware of the attack as dive-bombers drop bombs on the hangars at Ford Island which are well within sight of the ship.

0750-0755 |

As the bombs fall on Ford Island, three torpedoes strike the *Oklahoma* and it immediately begins to list to port. By the time of the final hit, she has heeled to an angle of 45 degrees.

With wrecks still smouldering in the background, rescuers cut holes in *Oklahoma* in an attempt to rescue trapped survivors. ✪

The upturned hull of *Oklahoma* can just be made out against the wall of smoke in the background pouring from the other vessels of Battleship Row. ✪

0757 |

Two or three additional torpedo strikes are felt and huge quantities of oil and water are displaced by the explosions.

0800 |

The anti-aircraft guns were manned almost immediately as the attack warning sounded, but the listing of the ship renders these entirely ineffective.

0810 |

It takes roughly eight to 10 minutes for the ship to turn over through an angle of about 135 degrees. Efforts to rescue trapped *Oklahoma* crew begin immediately, as do measures to try and salvage her.

0815 onwards |

It's reported that after *Oklahoma* has capsized, more than 60 officers make their way to the adjacent *Maryland* where they assist in the manning and service of anti-aircraft weapons.

BATTLESHIP ROW

1: USS *California*
Tennessee-class battleship
BB-44

OUTCOME

California was badly damaged by both Type 91 torpedoes and bombs and slowly sank to the bottom of the harbour in the subsequent days. Her salvage, repair and modernisation took longer than that of most of the ships at Pearl Harbor and the work was not complete until January 1944.

CREW LOST: 105

0755 |

Japanese fighters strafe the ship as they launch their attacks on the air facilities at Ford Island. The ship's company go promptly to their battle stations.

0805 |

The *California* crew open fire on Japanese aircraft but ammunition immediately available is limited. An order is given to get ammunition to the guns.

0805 |

Before the order can be carried out, three torpedoes strike the ship almost simultaneously with effects that are described as 'far reaching and disastrous'.

0820 |

An explosion shakes the vessel, floods the main radio compartment and causes fuel leaks.

Two different views show the vessel settling in Pearl Harbor after taking on water following a torpedo attack. ✪

A damaged *California* on Battleship Row. ✪

0830 |

California's machine gunners shoot down a Japanese dive-bomber which crashes in flames.

0830 |

A bomb penetrates the main deck and explodes on the second deck causing further flooding.

1002 |

Due to the enveloping fire from fuel and oil on the surface water, the order is given to temporarily abandon ship.

1015 |

With the flames clearing, the order to abandon ship is cancelled. Men return to man the battle stations of the slowly sinking ship, and begin salvage operations. Following repairs and overhaul, she was fully back in operations off the west coast by 1944.

0755 |

The *Tennessee* crew spot planes dropping bombs above Ford Island. Reports say they were immediately identified as Japanese by their markings.

0758 |

Bombs drop on the *Tennessee* causing a fire on Turret 3. Her crew are able to assess the damage done to other vessels on Battleship Row.

0930 |

The crew begins preparations to get *Tennessee* under way.

0930 |

The ship is ready to sail, but the surrounding fires from sinking battleships makes it almost impossible. By this time, the Japanese air attack has subsided.

Tennessee in between the sinking West Virginia, left, and the burning Arizona, right. ✪

2: USS *Maryland*
Colorado-class battleship
BB-46

OUTCOME

Moored on the shoreside of USS *Oklahoma*, *Maryland* received relatively minor damage during the Pearl Harbor attack, avoiding torpedo hits.

CREW LOST: 4

BATTLESHIP ROW

4: USS *Tennessee*
Tennessee-class battleship
BB-43

OUTCOME

Like USS *Maryland, Tennessee* was moored inboard of another ship – USS *West Virginia* – and so avoided torpedo attacks and instead only suffered bomb damage at the hands of the Japanese which affected two of her four gun turrets. She was also scorched by burning oil from the nearby USS *Arizona*. After temporary repairs she underwent a thorough modernisation and became a key vessel in the Pacific War and was part of the occupation force which followed Japan's surrender.

CREW LOST: 5

WITNESS STATEMENT

Seaman Leslie Vernon Short: "After breakfast on Sunday morning, I came to Group 'A' Machine Gun Station to write some letters home and address some Christmas cards. Suddenly I noticed planes diving on the air base nearby. At first I thought they were our planes just in mock diving practice attack but when I saw smoke and flames rise from a building, I looked closer and saw that they were not American planes.

"I broke out ammunition nearby, loaded my machine gun and opened fire on two torpedo planes coming in from the east which had just dropped two torpedoes. Flames and smoke burst from the first plane I aimed at, and it veered off to the left, falling toward the hospital. I think I also hit the second plane which I aimed at immediately after shooting at the first one but by then I was so busy that I cannot say for sure."

Maryland amid the smoke of Battleship Row, the capsized *Oklahoma* alongside. ✪

BATTLESHIP ROW

5: USS *West Virginia*
Colorado-class battleship
BB-48

OUTCOME

The Japanese assault was particularly brutal on the outboard moored USS *West Virginia*, which was struck by two bombs and at least seven torpedoes which blew gaping holes in her port side. Expert damage control prevented *West Virginia* from capsizing, but she quickly sank with more than 100 crew lost. During salvage in 1942, the bodies of 60 crewmen were found who had been trapped alive during the Pearl Harbor attack. In one compartment a calendar was found on which the days had been marked off up to and including December 23. The vessel underwent a complete overhaul in 1944 and came back – with a much-changed appearance – to take her place in the Pacific campaign.

CREW LOST: 106

WITNESS STATEMENT

Senior surviving officer R H Hillenkoetter: "The ship's batteries continued firing, and shortly after the Arizona explosion, the list on the West Virginia stopped and she gradually started to right herself. Meanwhile, efforts to push overboard the burning embers on the quarterdeck and to extinguish the fire on top of Turret 3 and in the planes was continued. There was another heavy shock, distinguishable from the shock of the ship's own guns firing, and it was reported that a large fire had broken out amidships.
"I went in to the deck-house and found the repair parties already working against a fire, but without much success, as the fire increased by leaps and bounds. At this time, a telephone talker said: 'Central station says abandon ship'. As it was evident the fire-fighting party had no chance to extinguish the fire, they were ordered to leave the ship. I went out on the port side of the quartered, and on seeing boats on that side went over to the starboard side. By this time the stern of the Tennessee was burning, and a wall of flame was advancing toward the West Virginia and the Tennessee from oil on the water from the Arizona. I looked around and saw no one else aft on deck and then I dove overboard and swam to the Tennessee.
"After the fires in the water were out, I went back by the pipe-line climbed up a Jacob's ladder to the forecastle of the Tennessee and went up on the bridge and reported to the commanding officer of that vessel. The West Virginia at this time was blazing furiously amidships, and the commanding officer, Tennessee, wanted to know if the magazines of the West Virginia were flooded. I assured him they were. Finding the greater part of the personnel of the West Virginia's battery on the Tennessee, I gave instructions that they were to remain on board under the orders of the Tennessee."

A boat rescues seamen from the stricken *West Virginia* as smoke fills the skies above. Two men can be seen still aboard on the superstructure. ✿

West Virginia and USS *Tennessee* are barely discernible as fuel and oil send clouds of smoke across their paths. ✪

Seamen tackle fires aboard *West Virginia* from the decks of the *Tennessee*. ✪

BATTLESHIP ROW

7: USS *Nevada*
Nevada-class battleship
BB-36

OUTCOME

USS *Nevada* was the only battleship able to get under way on December 7, and was headed out to sea. However, before she could move she was hit by a torpedo and two or three bombs and started to sink. To avoid going under in the narrow harbour entrance which would have left the facility unusable for an extended period of time, the *Nevada* crew deliberately beached her near Hospital Point. Despite heavy damage she was refloated in 1942 before undergoing extensive repairs and modernisation ahead of combat in the Second World War. As well as engagements in the Pacific, *Nevada* fired against German defences during the Normandy landings in June 1944.

CREW LOST: 57

Under way in the harbour, *Nevada* passes the dry docks as she heads for open waters. ✪

0801 |

Enemy aircraft are first observed and with a gun turret already armed and manned for routine fire control check the *Nevada* crew is able to quickly engage.

Looking over Ford Island Naval Station, *Nevada* is seen in the background after beaching. ✪

0802 |
Machine guns open fire and down a Japanese aircraft, but a bomber manages to drop a torpedo which strikes the port side bow.

0805-0830 |
Anti-aircraft fire is only intermittent as the onslaught subsides.

0830 |
A second heavy bomb attack means another fire breaks out, but during this time the crew have been able to make preparations to get *Nevada* under way.

0840 |
Nevada heads for the open water, but the torpedo strike and further bomb damage mean she is eventually grounded off Hospital Point to avoid sinking in the narrow harbour entrance.

Utah capsizing following the torpedo attack by Japanese Kate bombers. ✪

OTHER PACIFIC FLEET CASUALTIES

USS *Utah*, AG-16

During the first wave, 16 Kate bombers – armed with torpedoes – approached Ford Island from the north-west which was opposite Battleship Row. While the Japanese knew that aircraft carriers USS *Lexington* and USS *Saratoga* were not present, aircraft were still sent to find out whether either had unexpectedly returned and if they hadn't they could continue round to the south-east where the capital ships were moored and waiting.

It was soon confirmed that the carriers were not at present but the bomber crews did spot USS *Utah* – a former battleship, now auxiliary ship – which was used for target practice and was fitted with anti-aircraft training guns.

It made no sense for the Kates to hit the *Utah*, but two crews released their torpedoes and at 8.01am the first of these struck causing instant and serious flooding. Long timbers which were used to protect

Utah from the practice bombs which were dropped on her hindered damage control efforts and by 8.12am she had rolled on to her side. While some crewmembers managed to swim to shore, many more were trapped inside the capsized vessel. Using cutting equipment, survivors were able to rescue four fellow crewmembers but a total of 64 were lost, 58 of whom were entombed in the ship.

Given the acute detail which went into the planning of the Pearl Harbor attack, the bombing of an obsolete vessel seemed odd and US sailors speculated that the protective timbers had made the *Utah* look like an aircraft carrier which might explain why it was targeted. The mystery was solved when Japanese military were interviewed about the attack in the years after the war, explaining that a young pilot and his wingman mistook the *Utah* for an active battleship – not an aircraft carrier.

USS *Helena*, CL-50; USS *Oglala*, CM-4

The story of St Louis-class USS *Helena* is one of the old adage: wrong place, wrong time. At the moment of the Pearl Harbor attack, she was moored across the channel from Battleship Row – slightly to the west – in the berth that would have usually been occupied by USS *Pennsylvania* which was in the dry dock.

Helena's position meant she became a prime target for bombers who initially mistook her for the battleship and within three minutes of the first reports of the attack being relayed through the Pacific Fleet ships, a torpedo triggered a tremendous explosion which saw water immediately taken on board.

Damage control and counter-flooding meant that *Helena* remained afloat, but fire and smoke spread quickly throughout, killing many crewmembers and making even anti-aircraft operations difficult.

Helena is pictured undergoing repairs in dry dock on December 13. ✪

A view across Pearl Harbor shows capsized *Oglala* and listing Helena beyond. ✪

In total, 34 of *Helena's* crew lost their lives while a further 69 were wounded.

Tied, literally, to the fate of *Helena* was the minelayer USS *Oglala* – the flagship of the Pacific Fleet Mine Force – which was attached outboard of the light cruiser. The torpedoes which hit *Helena* blew holes in *Oglala* and she quickly took on water which could not be contained.

As it became clear that she would sink, *Oglala* was moved behind *Helena* to avoid compromising the warship by pinning her against the dock and, as predicted, about two hours after the explosion she rolled over and was submerged.

Salvage workers assess the capsized wreckage of *Oglala*. ✪

USS *Raleigh*, CL-7

Like the *Utah*, light-cruiser USS *Raleigh* was berthed on the east side of the north channel when the Japanese attacked.

And, also like the Utah, it's believed she was only targeted because bombers had taken a chance to fly over that portion of Pearl Harbor in case their information regarding the absence of US aircraft carriers was incorrect. Unlike the obsolete battleship, however, *Raleigh* was very much an active war vessel and as the first wave passed overhead a Kate aircraft fired two torpedoes, the second of which left a hole in her port side. The impact was such that it appeared *Raleigh* would capsize and all men not at guns were ordered to jettison topside weights and put both of the aircraft carried on board into the water.

Crewmen – none of whom were killed during the attack – managed to keep her upright and *Raleigh's* gunners were credited with the downing of five Japanese planes.

Raleigh is listing, but is just about kept afloat with the help of a barge lashed alongside. ✪

USS *Vestal*, AR-4

Navy repair ship USS *Vestal* was moored alongside the USS *Arizona* on December 7, lending its services to the battleship during a planned period of upkeep between December 6 and December 12.

As the Japanese air raid began, *Vestal* began firing its weapons arsenal but was almost immediately struck by two bombs intended for the more valuable vessels of Battleship Row. One struck the port side and penetrated three decks starting fires in the stores hold, while the second went through the entire ship leaving a 5ft hole in the bottom.

As the need to maintain the ship took precedence over manning guns, the fierce explosion which occurred on the *Arizona* blew men, equipment and structures from the *Vestal's* deck and promptly sent both her anti-aircraft gunners and commanding officer overboard.

Before Commander Cassin Young had swum back to the ship, the order to abandon her had been given.

While it appeared the ship could avoid being sunk, the surrounding fires from *Arizona* and the rest of Battleship Row would surely claim her so when he returned he rescinded the directive and attempted to get *Vestal* under way.

At 8.45am, the crew cut the mooring lines with axes and *Vestal* pulled away from the shoreline, escaping the consuming flames which were roaring from the wreckage of the *Arizona*. The ship was still taking on water, however, so at around

Vestal is shown beached at Aiea shoal after getting under way and escaping the engulfing flames of Battleship Row. ✪

9.10am she was anchored at a depth of 35ft off McGrew's Point. Citing the "unstable condition of the ship", Cassin made the decision to ground her at 9.50am; she was

damaged but fixable and played a vital role in the salvage and repair of the ships of the Pacific Fleet. Seven members of the crew were killed during the events of the day.

Hangars and aircraft aboard seaplane tender USS *Curtiss* which were damaged by a Japanese bomb. ✪

USS *Curtiss*, AV-4

USS *Curtiss* was a modern seaplane tender of the United States Navy, commissioned – a little more than a year before the Pearl Harbor attack – on November 15, 1940.

On the day of the Japanese offensive she was able to get under way almost immediately, firing at Japanese planes. However, *Curtiss's* early engagements were dominated by

submarines after her crew reported seeing a periscope and they gave chase.

Shortly after 9am, attention was turned back to the air as the Japanese second wave descended and *Curtiss's* gunners hit an aircraft which smashed into her number one crane and ignited fires on board.

Three minutes later the crew were targeting

Val dive-bombers when one dropped its payload in the area of the already damaged crane, exploding below deck and setting ablaze the main hangar.

Earlier strafing, the crash and the bomb left 21 crew dead but the survivors were able to extinguish the fires and set about immediate emergency repairs.

Scorched paintwork and other effects of fire damage can be seen on the forward hull of USS *Pennsylvania*. ✪

The dry dock: USS *Pennsylvania*, BB-38; USS *Cassin*, DD-372; USS *Downes*, DD-375

As B5N2 bombers launched their torpedoes on Battleship Row, one of its companions was across the channel and away to the west in dry dock.

USS *Pennsylvania* was undergoing routine maintenance when Japanese forces arrived, and because it was being worked on – and because initial strafing had targeted other ships closer to Ford Island – it was one of the first to open fire.

Due to its defences, the Kates failed in repeated attempts to torpedo the caisson of the dry dock which was the structure that ensured it remained watertight.

Bomb damage to the ship was minimal in comparison, but an explosion did wipe out a gun crew after a bomb hit her starboard side. The *Pennsylvania* lost 24 crew in total.

Enemy fire wasn't the only thing to affect her either: destroyers USS *Cassin* and USS *Downes* were both in the dry dock alongside and suffered far direr consequences as bombs exploded the latter's fuel tanks causing uncontrollable fires on both ships. *Pennsylvania* was scorched by the resulting flames and had a 1000lb torpedo tube from *Downes* blown into its forward deck.

The destroyers continued to burn and *Cassin* slipped from her keel blocks and rested against *Downes*, causing even further damage. In a bid to put out the fires there was a controlled flooding of the dry dock but the burning oil just rose with the water level and when ammunition on board the pair began to ignite and detonate they were both swiftly abandoned.

Both ships' hulls were damaged beyond repair, but much of their machinery and equipment was salvageable so brand-new vessels were eventually built around whatever could be rescued.

The jumbled wrecks of *Cassin* and *Downes* lay in front of *Pennsylvania*. ✪

An aerial view of Pearl Harbor on December 10 shows the amount of oil which has poured into the channel. On the left in dry dock is *Pennsylvania*, with the wrecks of *Cassin* and *Downes* in front. ✪

The moment the forward magazine of USS *Shaw* exploded is captured on camera. ✪

USS *Shaw*, DD-373

The most critical damage done to ships during the Pearl Harbor attack occurred during the first wave when Japanese Kate bombers utilised their torpedoes to devastating effect. The second wave, with dive-bombers swooping in at low altitudes, was perhaps a more intense period of action as engines roared just hundreds of feet above but it lacked the brutal impact of the initial groups. The only exception to this was the Mahan-Class destroyer USS *Shaw*.

Like the battleship USS *Pennsylvania* and fellow destroyers USS *Cassin* and USS *Downes*, *Shaw* was in dry dock – slightly further east along the shoreline of the

harbour – undergoing adjustments to her depth charge mechanisms.

As the Japanese bombers attempted to destroy the dry docks, *Shaw* took three hits and the armour-piercing payloads penetrated the outer structure of the ship, making their way down into its core.

Official reports in the aftermath described the bombs as 'liquid incendiary' devices, and while it's known that some Japanese weaponry did have chemical elements designed to burn there was doubt cast over this hypothesis and it was suggested that instead *Shaw's* forward fuel tanks had been ruptured by the blasts.

Whether the truth is one, the other, or a combination of both, the bombs sparked an all-consuming fire which ripped through the forward part of ship. The blaze spread far too quickly for the crew to have any chance of tackling it and by 9.25am all fire-fighting facilities had been exhausted and the order to abandon ship was given.

Seamen attempted to flood the dry dock and while it had some success in negating the situation on the surface, within the ship itself the fire was burning more fiercely by the second. Shortly after 9.30am, the forward magazine of the *Shaw* exploded.

The incredible force of the blast separated the bow from the rest of the ship, with the exception of the keel structure and the damage done, first by the bombs and then by the explosion, caused the dock itself to sink. Pieces of debris anywhere between one and six inches in diameter rained down reaching as far as half-a-mile away.

Because this occurred more than an hour-and-a-half after hostilities had begun, cameras were being used to record events and images of the explosion would become among the most iconic of the attack, and the most revealing as to the sheer scale of what had happened.

A strong wind from the stern and 'the strenuous efforts of the remaining personnel' was all that saved *Shaw* from being savaged and gutted by fire as happened to *Cassin* and *Downes*. The ship was at sea again by February of 1942, an incredible feat belying the attack and subsequent devastation it had endured which claimed the lives of 24 crewmembers.

A photograph from Ford Island shows a different angle of the blast. ✪

A view from behind *Shaw* shows smoke billowing from her forward structure as fires rage within. ✪

Not only did the explosion destroy the bow of *Shaw*, but it also left the floating dry dock in a state of ruin. ✪

As airmen survey the extent of the damage at Ford Island Naval Air Station, *Shaw* explodes across the harbour. ✪

Two huge columns of smoke pour from ships at Pearl Harbor. On the right is *Shaw*, and on the left the destroyer *Helena*. ✪

The wrecked *Shaw* – bow completely destroyed – sits in the floating dry dock. The fires have nearly gone out, but smoke still rises from the structure. ✪

CHAPTER 13

JAPANESE MIDGET SUBMARINES

The facts, the theories, the mystery

For many years the accepted version of events is that it was Japanese aircraft which decimated America's capital ships, but what of the five midget submarines which were in the water on December 7, 1941?

LENGTH 330 FT

A STANDARD FIRST CLASS JAPANESE SUBMARINE COMPARED WITH THE TWO-MAN TYPE.

PHOTOGRAPH OF JAPANESE TWO-MAN SUBMARINE DAMAGED AND BEACHED AFTER ATTACK ON HONOLULU.

STEERING AND DIVING GEAR

AFTER TRIMMING AND COMPENSATING TANKS

ENGINEER

CONNING TOWER

ELECTRIC PROPULSION MOTOR

OFFICER AT CONTROLS

EXPLOSIVE CHARGE

ENGINEER'S LOCKER

COMPRESSED AIR BOTTLES

PORT BALLAST TANK

18 IN TORPEDO IN LAUNCHING TUBE

BATTERY TANK

THESE SMALL SUBMARINES HAVE TO BE CARRIED IN MOTHER-SHIP TO WITHIN 100 MILES OF THEIR OBJ

PORT BALLAST TANK

OXYGEN BOTTLES

FORWARD TRIMMING AND COMPENSATING TANKS

This US government illustration of a Japanese midget submarine was created based on the study of a vessel that was grounded on an Oahu beach the day after the Pearl Harbor attack. ✪

GH DAVIS 1941

In the early 1940s, as Japan prepared for potential conflict in the Pacific, its navy made huge strides in the field of submarine building and was able to develop midget vessels as advanced as anything any other nation in the world could offer.

The first examples of these remarkable machines weighed around 50 tonnes, could be operated by a crew of two and were able to carry a fearsome duo of 1000lb torpedoes, weaponry of far greater destructive force than the payload of the bombers involved in the Pearl Harbor attack. They were quick, too, and at a top speed of 19 knots they could outpace several of the standard naval types of the day.

To ensure their technology could not be harnessed by others, few details of their construction were available and their missions were shrouded in secrecy, even to the point where the individual vessels were not numbered or named. Instead they tended to be known by the designation of the larger submarine which was responsible for transporting them on long voyages.

Such journeys are exactly what occurred in the weeks before the Pearl Harbor attack as five Japanese fleet submarines – *I-16*, *I-18*, *I-20*, *I-22* and *I-24* – left Kure Naval District on November 25 and joined the Pearl Harbor strike force, each carrying a midget sub.

So new was the midget submarine project that the five types were attached to their 'mother ship' by hastily fashioned leather straps; the fact that they survived the perilous journey across the Pacific is a remarkable feat in itself.

As the five larger submarines approached Oahu they slowed, eventually stopping around 12 miles from the mouth of Pearl Harbor shortly before midnight of December 7. Just after, at around 1am, the five midget subs detached and set their course for the US naval base with their stated mission to lie in wait and destroy any American ships which attempted to escape the harbour once the air attack had begun.

With the midget submarines' batteries only providing power for a matter of hours, their instructions would take them into the heart of the battle with no concrete plan in place to return. As the 10 crewmen closed in on the channel entrance, they had to accept the notion that they might well have to sacrifice their lives.

What they did or did not accomplish that day has been, and still is, debatable. Extensive research has led to near-conclusive proof about what became of four of them, but the fate of the fifth midget submarine remains somewhat of a mystery. Because its movements and actions on December 7 are still unknown, and will perhaps never be proven, one persistent question continues to go unanswered: was a Japanese midget submarine responsible for sinking a vessel on Battleship Row?

Crewmembers of USS *Ward* pose in front of the gun that fired the first shots of the Pacific War. ✪

Midget submarine #1

It was a calm and peaceful night in the waters around Oahu as Wickes-class destroyer USS *Ward* – DD-139 – undertook a routine precautionary patrol off the coast. At 3.57am the minesweeper USS *Condor*, also at sea around the island, reported a visual sighting of a periscope and notified the *Ward*, which investigated immediately.

An initial sweep turned up nothing and the *Ward* – although on alert – returned to her normal patrol duties. Then came a second sighting, this time from the cargo ship USS *Antares* whose crew radioed in that they were being tailed by what they believed to be a non-American vessel which looked like a small submarine trying to follow it through the anti-submarine nets at the channel entrance.

It's unclear, even today, whether *Condor* and *Antares* saw the same sub.

Ward was much closer this time and was able to respond swiftly. Firing guns one and three her crew believed they scored a hit

with the second salvo somewhere between the hull and conning tower, and to be sure she dropped depth charges. Witnesses on deck say the submarine rolled and sank before a significant amount of oil was seen on the surface. Little did they know they had just fired the first American shots of the Second World War.

The developments were radioed to base and the message was passed from department to department, but because reports of submarine sightings had become relatively commonplace off the coast of Hawaii little more than cursory notice was paid. At approximately the same time that news of the skirmish reached the head of the Pacific Fleet, Admiral Husband Kimmel, the first reports of Japanese planes being spotted over Pearl Harbor were already coming through.

Had more been made of the submarine sinking, there is a possibility that crew aboard the fleet's ships and military personnel on the ground could have been on higher alert, but given that it took place

just over an hour before aircraft arrived it's unlikely that any kind of significant preparations for the Japanese offensive could have been made in that time.

In the chaotic aftermath of December 7, the question lingered as to whether or not *Ward* had actually sunk the midget submarine. The fact that no wreckage could be found left doubts as to whether she had actually even engaged one.

It would take more than 65 years to find what is now widely accepted to be midget submarine number one when – on August 28, 2002 – a team from the University of Hawaii finally located the sunken vessel 1200ft below the surface. Discovered between three and four miles from the entrance to Pearl Harbor, not only does the location tally with the report from *Ward*, but the submarine's conning tower bears a hole which matches the calibre of its artillery.

Crucially, both of the submarine's torpedoes were found still in their tubes; midget submarine number one had definitely not fired on American ships.

USS *Condor*, the first American vessel to sight a submarine in the early hours of December 7. ✪

USS *Ward* was finally able to locate a Japanese submarine after USS *Antares*, shown, reported it was being followed by an unidentified vessel. ✪

USS *Current* raises midget submarine number two from Keehi Lagoon in 1960. ✪

Midget submarine #2

A little like number one, the actions of midget submarine number two on the day of the Pearl Harbor attack are not known. What is certain though is that it was sunk by a depth charge in Keehi Lagoon – an inlet to the east between Pearl Harbor and the Hawaiian city of Honolulu.

In the years after the attack, as theories began to swirl about the possibility of submarine torpedo attacks, US Navy divers recovered the wreck of midget number two in June of 1960 and found that both torpedoes were still aboard. It's unlikely that it had ever been in Pearl Harbor and it had certainly not fired on Battleship Row.

Once the torpedoes had been neutralised, the salvaged vessel returned to Japan where it was restored and put on permanent display outside Japan's Naval Academy in Etajima.

The wreck of vessel number two is brought ashore by American navy personnel. ✪

Kazuo Sakamaki was the first prisoner of the Pacific War when he was captured on Oahu after escaping midget submarine number three. He's pictured in 1956 outside the Toyota plant in Tokyo where he worked after returning to Japan. He would later recall that he received better treatment from his American guards than he did from old neighbours when he returned home. *Courtesy, PA*

Midget submarine #3

As the five midget submarines headed for Pearl Harbor, a malfunctioning gyrocompass on vessel number three caused the crew several difficulties with navigation and they began to veer away from their intended destination.

Quite literally lost at sea, she was caught twice on reefs, both times drawing fire from several US patrol vessels. She finally grounded on Waimanalo Beach on the eastern shore of Oahu the following day, more than 30 miles from the entrance to Pearl Harbor.

Capture was not an option for Japanese soldiers and sailors; were it to appear likely that they would be taken prisoner they were honour-bound to take their own lives – particularly submarine crews who were under an obligation to protect the technology of the vessels by destroying

A journalist is given the opportunity to inspect the captured submarine at Mare Island in California where the US Navy has had it brought in order to examine it. *Courtesy, PA*

Midget submarine number three is hauled ashore by US military personnel the day after the Pearl Harbor attack. ○

them so they couldn't be examined by enemy forces.

Kazuo Sakamaki, however, swam ashore and was captured by Hawaii National Guard Corporal David Akui; the submarine's commanding officer becoming the first prisoner of the Pacific War.

Sakamaki became a figure of shame in his homeland after he allowed himself to be captured by the enemy, but it later emerged he requested the permission of his captors to commit suicide on several occasions as he attempted to fulfil his duty.

As for whether submarine three could have fired upon Battleship Row: it never even got close to Pearl Harbor and was still armed with both torpedoes when it was hauled in by US forces.

Midget submarine #4

The only Japanese vessel known to have definitely found a way past America's anti-submarine defences to enter Pearl Harbor, midget submarine number four did manage to fire its two torpedoes at American ships.

It wasn't Battleship Row that it targeted, however, but the USS *Curtiss* which was in the north channel on the opposite side of Ford Island to where USS *Arizona* and company were moored. An initial torpedo strike missed its target, hitting a reef. American destroyer USS *Monaghan* came to the aid of the seaplane tender and narrowly avoided the second torpedo launch before ramming submarine four and dropping depth charges against it.

The damage sunk the vessel almost immediately, and in the shallow waters of Pearl Harbor the wreck was recovered shortly after the day of the attack. It was used as fill during an expansion of Pearl Harbor's submarine base, was dug up in 1952, and then reburied almost immediately. The remains of the two crewmen are still on board.

BELOW: The wreck of midget sub number four which was sunk by the American destroyer USS *Monaghan.* ○

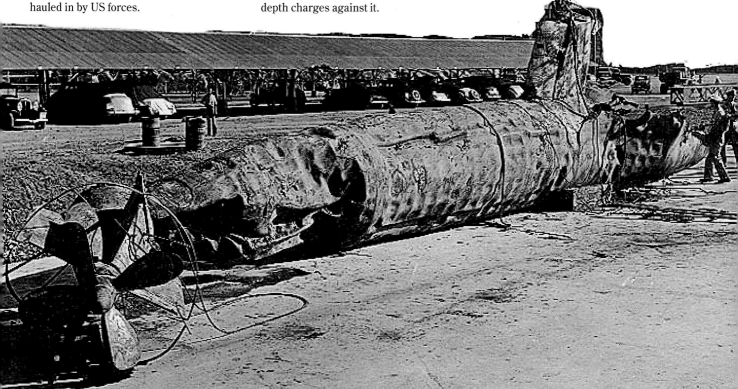

Midget submarine #5

In 1999, 2000 and 2001, research teams found three different parts of a Japanese midget submarine lying in the waters off Pearl Harbor. How it got there and why it was in three sections caused a great deal of confusion, as did the fact it was found among several American amphibious landing craft.

It appears the answer lies in an event which occurred on May 21, 1944, known as the West Loch Disaster. An accidental explosion at a staging area for US landing ships caused a fire and subsequent damage to several American vessels and vehicles, as well as the deaths of more than 100 US service personnel.

With operations in the Pacific ongoing, the navy quashed all news of the incident and quickly set about recovering the sunken ships and other machinery from the harbour, preparing to have it dumped out in the ocean.

During the salvage mission, divers discovered the remains of midget submarine number five and, although records are sketchy because of the enforced secrecy, it appears as if the wreck was found in two sections before the bigger part was dismantled into a more manageable piece so it could be littered across the Hawaiian sea bed with the rest of the mangled metal. The pieces still lie where they were left that day.

If the submarine was sunk, or scuttled by its own crew to avoid capture, in the West Loch where it was originally discovered then it had entered Pearl Harbor and could have fired on Battleship Row.

It's entirely possible that the torpedoes were removed during the salvage, but analysis of the tubes suggests this is unlikely due to the nature of the bacterial growth which has since covered the metal. It's a fairly certain conclusion that submarine five did in fact fire. What it fired against is uncertain.

With experts as sure as they can be that midget submarines one to four didn't launch torpedoes against Battleship Row, it could only be vessel number five which engaged one or more of America's capital ships.

In 1999, an article published by the United States Naval Institute presented evidence, using a famous photograph from the Pearl Harbor attack – right, that a midget submarine did in fact fire torpedoes at USS *West Virginia* and USS *Oklahoma* and contributed to the sinking of the pair. Its authors are certainly convinced that a torpedo strike makes sense with regard to the speed at which *Oklahoma* capsized, given that submarine torpedoes were armed with a warhead roughly 70% more powerful than those dropped by the Kate bombers.

While it was and remains a controversial theory, at the time there were enough unaccounted-for torpedoes for this to be possible alongside reports from the captain of light cruiser USS *St Louis* in the aftermath of the attack who was certain his ship was fired upon by a midget sub as she broke out of the harbour between 9.30am and 10am. The two torpedoes, he insisted, exploded against a submerged reef before reaching him and his crew.

In the time since, the other four wrecks have been located which means if they did come from midget submarines, then only one of these accounts can be right. One other possibility is that a Japanese fleet submarine had moved close enough to Pearl Harbor to launch its own torpedo strike – but no such records of this have ever been found in the Imperial Japanese Navy archives.

Supporting the idea that either *Oklahoma* or *West Virginia* was hit is the fact that Japanese forces received a radio message from a midget sub just after midnight of December 8 in which came the word 'kira'. In Morse code, it would only have taken a slightly extended dot for the first letter to mistakenly send 'kira' instead of 'tora' – the signal that the submarine had achieved its aim of destroying an American ship.

That's certainly the way it was interpreted in Japan and the nine submarine crewmen – excluding Sakamaki – became wartime celebrities and godlike figures in their home country for courageously giving their lives in the name of destroying a mighty American battleship. It was certainly a jump from one simple and incorrect word, but the story stuck.

While having logic on its side, the Battleship Row theory is a theory, and the interpretation of the photograph has to stand up against the ironclad belief and eyewitness account of *St Louis* skipper George Rood who maintained the vessel was fired upon.

Other possible explanations for the rooster-tail spray in the below image are falling debris or anti-aircraft fire, reflection or shadows, or possibly just the natural

Researchers from the United States Naval Institute believe that this rooster-tail - the name given to the unique plume of water that is fired into the air when a submarine propeller breaks the surface - is from Japanese midget submarine number five. They posit that as it fired its one-ton torpedoes, the weight displaced from its front section would have forced its tail to lift violently, forcing the propeller out of the water.

interaction of waves caused by the ripples from falling bombs and aerial torpedoes. None of the reports on the damaged or destroyed US ships suggest anything as powerful as a 1000lb torpedo had struck them either, and subsequent exploration of the *Arizona* has found no evidence of such torpedo attacks.

Nearly 75 years on from the events of December 7 and it's not even known for sure that Japanese midget submarine number five did indeed fire its torpedoes. The evidence suggests it did, but then a wider question emerges – what did if fire against, and were the strikes successful? Did the final two torpedoes crash against a reef as they hurtled toward USS *St Louis*? Had a Japanese midget submarine managed to hide in plain sight just off Ford Island during the attack? Perhaps it's neither of these and the truth lies down an entirely different path.

In scenes reminiscent of the Pearl Harbor attack, smoke pours from the landing ship area on the shoreline of the West Loch after an accidental explosion caused fires to rip through several US vessels and vehicles. ✪

A conclusive answer is far from forthcoming, and it would seem that for now, and the foreseeable future, it's up to the individual to look at the collection of facts and varying theories, and make a decision for themselves.

A famous image from the Pearl Harbor attack that some believe uncovers the vital clues needed to finally reveal what happened to Japanese midget submarine number five. ✪

Waves and what appears to be fuel and oil around the USS *West Virginia* would indicate that it has just been struck; but was a Japanese midget submarine responsible?

It's also argued that at least one of the streaks coming from the proposed location of submarine is a torpedo trail which is headed in the direction of USS *West Virginia*.

CHAPTER 14

JAPAN 'DECLARES' WAR AGAINST AMERICA

Chaos and controversy

In 1941 international law dictated that any aggressor wishing to attack a neutral nation had to explicitly declare war beforehand. Prior to Pearl Harbor, there was no such warning of hostilities from Japan to the American government...

On December 7 at 9pm, Washington DC time, nearly 10 hours since the attack on Pearl Harbor commenced, the American embassy in Tokyo received a formal notification announcing war.

The time difference meant it was already 11am on December 8 in Japan and the story was printed on the front pages of its newspapers that day.

The fact that the official declaration came so long after the attack, and that it had not occurred ahead of it, caused consternation among the highest offices of the American government. Not only had the events of the day been the bloodiest ever inflicted on the US by a foreign power but – in the eyes of Roosevelt and his administration – it had been a sneak attack.

The question of why and how Japan failed to notify the US before the bombs began to fall has been debated ever since. Some argue that it was a deliberate act of treachery aimed at maintaining the secrecy of Japan's military plans, while others suggest that it was incompetence on the part of Japanese officials and war was meant to be declared but it simply did not happen in time. Another theory suggests that Japan's military exerted its considerable influence and power to delay the delivery of its government's message. The truth probably lies somewhere between all three.

The military makes its move

In September 1941, the Japanese military decided that war was a real and very possible option and, as training for an attack in the Pacific got under way, discussion began as to how, when and even if Japan should notify the US of its hostile intentions.

Many high-ranking naval officials, most notably Chief of Staff Nagano, were against a declaration given that the element of surprise was so crucial to the imperial army's plans. Part of his strategy was for Japanese diplomats to continue negotiations with their American counterparts and

More than half-a-century after the Pearl Harbor attack, documents were discovered that show Foreign Minister Shigenori Togo had drafted a formal declaration of war for Japan to deliver to the United States. It never reached its intended recipient. ○

maintain the illusion that a settlement could be found which avoided all-out war.

Admiral Yamamoto agreed with Nagano that talks should continue as a veil, but was of the belief that Japan should issue a formal notice of war before launching the attack as a matter of honour and integrity.

In the battle of Yamamoto versus Nagano, it was the junior Yamamoto who prevailed as Foreign Minister Shigenori Togo came down in favour of adhering to the stipulations set out by the Hague III Convention on the Opening of Hostilities which stated 'hostilities should not commence without previous warning' and that either an unconditional declaration of war should be made, or a conditional declaration coupled with an ultimatum.

In English language documents discovered in 1997 – the Japanese originals were later uncovered – it emerged that Togo did indeed act on his belief and issued a formal declaration of war which

was signed and later verified by secretary Toshikazu Kase. For reasons unknown the unconditional and explicit notification of impending conflict remained hidden in the foreign ministry's historical archive for 55 years and instead it was a lengthy and ambiguous memorandum that was delivered to US Secretary of State Cordell Hull.

The Hull Note

At the same time as military leaders in Japan were pushing enthusiastically for war and debating how they would go about announcing it, throughout 1941 there was still a desire for peace from within the governments of both countries.

The fact that negotiations were ongoing – even after the decision had been taken to attack – was not just to disguise the mobilisation of Japanese forces but was a genuine attempt to avoid a war that both knew would be costly and which neither felt entirely prepared for.

Japanese Prime Minister Fumimaro Konoe had strived for a settlement throughout the year and a meeting between himself and Roosevelt nearly came to fruition twice – one proposed in Honolulu and another in mainland America.

In what would become a critical move during the lead-up to the events of December 7, Konoe's authority was washed away as Army Minister Hideki Tojo announced that a deadline for a breakthrough – which had been set as October 14 – had passed and the prime minister had failed in his task.

Unable to win backing from the navy, Konoe resigned on October 16 and was replaced by Tojo – the army supremo now head of Japan's government. On forming his cabinet, Tojo assured Hirohito he would make a final attempt to reach terms with the US, but if that couldn't be achieved by December 1 then conflict was the only option remaining. Japan's ambassador to the US, Kichisaburo Nomura, was instructed

With military leader Hideki Tojo at the head of the Japanese government, the country moved closer to war in the Pacific Theatre. ✪

to present final proposals – Plans A and B. The former fell on deaf ears as there was no commitment to troop withdrawal from China included. Plan B had more promise as it outlined a possible Japanese retreat in Indochina and a vow not to move into Thailand, Malaya, Singapore or the Dutch East Indies. Still, apart from a somewhat loose pledge to explore talks with the Chinese government, there was no budging on the suspension of its military operations there.

To further compound matters, military agencies had uncovered Japanese secret communications which showed they planned even further expansion. Plan B was presented on November 20 with a response being requested by November 29.

The US was aware that while these talks were ongoing, Japan was in the advanced stages of planning for a full-scale war in the Pacific should they come to nothing and believed hostilities would begin within days of the talks ending.

On November 26 Hull presented Nomura with the Hull note – America's response to Plan B – and one of its absolute conditions was the complete removal of Japanese

troops from China. Tojo told his cabinet that the demands were tantamount to an ultimatum, and argued the case that the US had, in essence, issued its own declaration of war – they had no choice but to respond.

In the eyes of international law, Hull's statement did not call for a cessation of negotiations and Japan had the alternative option of ceding to American demands; it was, therefore, not a declaration. The prime minster took a different stance and on December 1, as planned and with the forces already under way, Hirohito approved attacks against the United States, Great Britain and the Netherlands to take place in their respective Pacific territories.

On December 6, with little more than suggestive intelligence that an offensive might be likely, Roosevelt telegraphed a personal message to Emperor Hirohito in which he called for the two nations to avoid the 'tragic possibilities' which war in the Pacific could bring. Had the emperor wanted to pull back his forces, it seems unlikely that at this point he could have restrained his military, which was closing in on Hawaii.

The Fourteen-Part Message

In the hours before the bombers and fighters descended on Pearl Harbor, American code breakers started to unravel fragments of a 5000-word transmission from Tokyo to the Japanese embassy in the US. The content was what would become known as the Fourteen-Part Message, as it was sent and then deciphered in 14 stages.

Deciding that it should adhere to conventional thinking, Japan intended the memo to be a declaration of war which would be delivered to Hull 30 minutes prior to the attack; in the end it achieved neither of those aims.

Having uncovered 13 of the 14 parts of the message and other communications, US officials became aware that Nomura was under instruction to officially deliver it to the secretary of state at 1pm in Washington,

DC and that its contents laid out Japan's opposition to further negotiations.

With the importance placed on the 1pm meeting, the US War Department issued an alert to its Pacific territories – including Hawaii – realising that the corresponding time there would be early morning, ideal for a surprise offensive.

Unfortunately, radio contact with Hawaii was temporarily disrupted and so the warning was sent via a commercial telegraph. It would reach Oahu at noon, more than two hours after Japanese planes had vacated the skies above.

The 14th part was finally revealed but it contained no official statement of intent, just that the 'hope to preserve and promote the peace of the Pacific through cooperation with the American government has finally been lost'. It suggested diplomatic relations were at an end, but nothing more.

As 1pm in Washington approached, Nomura delayed his meeting with Hull to 1.45pm before he and special envoy Saburo Kurusu arrived at 2.05pm and were received at 2.20pm. The timing here is crucial, because at the point Nomura placed the message in the hand of Hull, the secretary of state was already receiving briefings informing him that his country was under attack. There were two significant issues which caused the delay: the late decision to deliver the message to Hull in Washington rather than American ambassador Joseph Grew in Tokyo, and the time it took for the Japanese embassy to decode and then translate the message to English.

The fact remains, however, that even if the memo had reached Hull before or at 1pm, it would have done little to indicate to him that Japan had changed its stance and declared war. While there was growing concern about a Japanese attack in the Pacific and intelligence which suggested Pearl Harbor was a target, it is this fact which meant the events of December 7 could officially be declared a surprise attack, with Roosevelt going to war on that basis.

US Secretary of State Cordell Hull who delivered the famous Hull note which Japan treated as an American ultimatum. ✪

The headline on the front page of the *Gettysburg Times'* December 8 edition summarises the diplomatic events of the previous day. ✪

US Navy sailors honour friends and colleagues who were killed at Naval Air Station Kaneohe during the Pearl Harbor attack. ✪

THE AFTERMATH

America reels, reacts and retaliates

Within 24 hours of the Pearl Harbor attack, the US had responded to Japan's declaration of war with one of their own. What was meant to be a crippling pre-emptive strike was instead the action which unshackled America from the chains of isolationism...

The grim reality of the Pearl Harbor attack hits home with images such as this; a deceased US sailor washes up on a beach following the events of December 7. ✪

A 1938 Ford ambulance riddled with shrapnel holes at Ewa Field. ✪

US military personnel stand outside a Pearl Harbor medical dispensary on December 8. The day before, this location would have been inundated with wounded sailors, soldiers and civilians. ✪

A s Japan drew its Pearl Harbor offensive to a conclusion, the military forces and residents on Oahu were left in a state of confusion and shock. Medical personnel desperately tried to help wounded sailors and civilians, often having to prioritise those who had a chance of survival over individuals whose injuries were too severe.

On what was meant to be a calm and quiet Sunday morning, the cold and hard brutality of war had descended on Hawaii and the body count began to pile up. In makeshift hospitals and operating theatres, doctors and nurses marked the foreheads of patients to denote their condition – C, critically injured; F, fatally wounded; M, morphine administered. When the felt tip pens ran out, nurses resorted to using lipstick. In the water, sailors became rescue workers as they tackled raging fires and made attempts to free trapped colleagues, friends and brothers from sunken vessels. Many of the dead would come from the destroyed ships, killed either by explosions and fires or after becoming entombed in what effectively became steel coffins.

Acting on years of training and basic instinct, many experienced commanders and officers realised that, even with the bullets still firing and bombs dropping around them, if they could stabilise the less-damaged ships early there was every chance of salvaging them from the shallow waters of Pearl Harbor and efforts were made with this aim in mind.

While these chaotic scenes ensued at ground level the skies above continued to be peppered with anti-aircraft fire and flak bursts as American gunners maintained a state of full battle readiness. There were several incidents of US planes being hit by friendly fire as the forces at Pearl Harbor laid in wait for further Japanese aggression.

In the wider world, news of the attack spread back throughout mainland America sparking a dangerous combination of consternation, anger and resolve. The events of the previous decade in both Europe and Asia had chipped away at the isolationism movement for more than a decade, but it took a mere hour-and-a-half on the morning of December 7, 1941, to wash it away for good.

The third wave that never was

The immediate concern for those at Pearl Harbor in the wake of the initial destruction was whether or not they were still under attack after Japanese planes had vacated the skies above. While the base's defences had put up a much greater fight against the Japanese force during the second wave, the devastation was such that any further assault would have surely resulted in considerable damage.

However, of all the myths and misconceptions that have arisen in the time since the Pearl Harbor attack, the idea that Japan mistakenly decided against launching a third wave once its first- and second-wave aircraft returned to the carriers is perhaps the most persistent.

The force had just completed one of the most carefully constructed military operations in history; a ground-breaking carrier-based attack on a scale which had never been seen before. Commander of the strike force Admiral Nagumo was never likely to abandon a detailed two-wave battle plan to send his pilots back towards Hawaii unprepared and without exact and comprehensive objectives. He did not even consider it.

So why has the notion that a decision was taken not to embark on a third wave become so entrenched in the overall Pearl Harbor narrative? In the months and years after the attack it became clear that while Japan achieved its stated objectives with incredible success, there were serious flaws in the original plan.

As a nation which was itself being strangled by a lack of resources, Japan inexplicably failed to target fuel and oil reserves at Pearl Harbor – vitally important to a mammoth Pacific Fleet which was more than 2000 miles away from the US west coast. Unbeknownst to the Japanese, US officers at Pearl Harbor were concerned by the vulnerability of their fuel storage tanks to strikes from the air and had begun construction of an underground facility. It would not have been easy for Japanese machine gunners to penetrate the reinforced tanks, but bomb damage might have been enough to cause an explosion or fire which could well have been devastating.

Japanese bombs hit several American capital vessels, but repair ships, dockyards and on-shore storage and maintenance facilities were ignored. Salvage was not only possible, but likely, and Japan had done little to affect the ability of the fleet to continue operating out of Pearl Harbor in the weeks, months or years to come.

And holes in Japan's intelligence gathering meant that none of the prized US aircraft carriers were in port on the day of the launch.

These critical errors in the tactical planning of the Pearl Harbor attack have been neatly wrapped up into a theory that each could, should and would have been rectified had Nagumo sent the aircraft at his disposal back into action, but it simply

Had Pearl Harbor's fuel storage been successfully targeted it could have caused untold damage and devastation. ✪

doesn't fit with the facts.

The first major obstacle to the idea of a third wave is the fact the carrier fleet was only ever primed for the planned two stages. Supplies – most vitally fuel – were not plentiful given the lengthy journey which had been undertaken halfway across the Pacific, and there was little chance it could sustain the trip home had it been required to hold its position for the indefinite duration of an extended attack.

Furthermore, throughout the 18 months of planning prior to launch the main creators of the Pearl Harbor offensive had stressed how vital the element of surprise would be to its success. With the initial attack meeting this key objective, any subsequent wave could not possibly have done so with the American forces now fully expecting more Japanese planes to arrive.

Most significantly, Japanese strategists believed – however misguidedly – that because they had been able to attack without prior warning and inflict damage to American ships as they had intended, their objective to strike such a blow to US morale and confidence that war would be short or avoided altogether had been comprehensively met. There was simply no valid reason to risk the large force which it had managed to secretly muster in the waters north of Hawaii.

It was later claimed that two of Yamamoto's right-hand-men, Fuchida and Genda, urged Nagumo to carry out a third strike and its reported that the captains of the other carriers were prepared and willing to do so. It must be remembered, however, that Genda was an advocate of a Hawaiian invasion and his enthusiasm for further action has likely been exaggerated through the years.

Indeed, the morning after the attack Yamamoto supported the fact that no third wave had been launched – and it was only later, with the benefit of hindsight, when Pearl Harbor's architect said it had been a great mistake not to consolidate Japanese success with a further assault.

"A day which will live in infamy"

As fears of further death and destruction subsided in Hawaii and people began the long process of coming to terms with what had occurred, the full extent of the events of the morning began to filter through to Washington, DC and President Roosevelt.

In a world long before 24-hour TV news and other digital media platforms it was radio which was the dominant source of current affairs information and it was over the airwaves that the American public first began to learn of the dramatic developments which were unfolding.

Given that it was already afternoon on the east coast, many of the bulletins announcing the Pearl Harbor attack broke in to Sunday's traditional American football games with one report coming from a newsman on the rooftop of a building in Honolulu; his stark words, 'It is no joke. It is a real war', summing up the evident feeling of surprise.

At the White House, press secretary Stephen Early and his assistant Ruthjane Rumelt relayed pieces of the story to the gathered and rapidly expanding press corps as they emerged, while outside worried crowds gathered at the gates looking for updates and reassurance.

It was a scene mirrored in towns and cities across the land as citizens took to the streets in a bid to get up-to-speed on the details. It would take most of the rest of the day for the full story to emerge, and when it did the tale was a harrowing one; more than 2000 sailors were either confirmed killed or were unaccounted for, with more than 1000 wounded. The shockwaves rippled across the nation.

By the following morning, the attack had galvanised public opinion firmly in favour of intervention in the Second World War with few dissenting voices left as the president made his way to Capitol Hill to deliver a speech to a joint session of Congress in which he was expected to request a vote on a formal declaration.

What followed has become one of the most famous, recognisable and iconic pieces

President Franklin D Roosevelt delivers his famous Infamy Speech to a joint session of the United States Congress in Washington, DC. *Courtesy, PA*

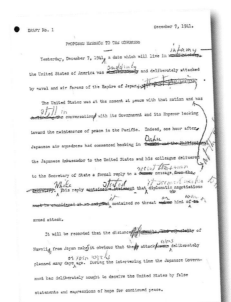

A first draft of the Infamy Speech shows how the memorable line was not in the original. Roosevelt replaced the words 'world history' with 'infamy' as the final content of the message was decided. ○

of American rhetoric ever delivered when, in the opening line of his address, Roosevelt declared December 7, 1941, to be 'a date which will live in infamy'.

His statement was brief and hard-hitting, aimed at conveying the shock and horror felt by all Americans and emphasising the attack as a dastardly, dishonest and unprovoked assault on US liberty and freedom which had been carried out while Japan had pursued phoney diplomatic negotiations as a ruse.

The seven-minute masterpiece of oratory had the desired effect and 33 minutes later Congress overwhelmingly moved to declare war on Japan with only one representative – the pacifist Jeannette Ranking – voting against the motion.

In the days after, army recruiting stations were inundated with volunteers wanting to sign-up to fight, with crowds reported to be twice the size of those that had formed when Americans answered

Journalists based at the White House rush to begin filing reports as news of the Pearl Harbor attack starts to come through. ○

Crowds gather in New York City's Times Square to read news bulletins about the Pearl Harbor attack which are flashed up on the electric board. *Courtesy, PA*

A US government propaganda poster urged citizens to 'Avenge December 7'. ✪

Volunteers for military service stretch around the block as they queue outside a recruitment centre. Similar scenes were witnessed across the country in the days after the Pearl Harbor attack. ✪

the call to war in 1917. Isolationism hadn't just been put to one side, it had collapsed entirely in the face of the one event which had always been capable of challenging it: a direct assault by a foreign aggressor on the American way of life.

Roosevelt's narrative of America refusing to cower to a despicable enemy force which would attempt to destroy it through a heinous sneak attack became the norm and was the basis for a series of propaganda

messages which centred on the slogan: Remember December 7.

The desire for war did not need compounding, but as Japanese forces followed the Pearl Harbor attack with a series of swift and decisive military victories throughout South East Asia it hardened America's stance. American forces were not yet prepared for war, while British, Australian and Dutch forces were drained after two years of conflict

already. All were powerless to resist and by the summer of 1942 Japan had captured Thailand, Hong Kong, Burma, the Dutch East Indies, New Guinea, Malaya, the Philippines, Singapore, Bali and Timor, and had struck against Australia.

In the face of Japanese expansion and after the debilitating strike on Pearl Harbor, America was meant to back down and negotiate a settlement. Japan had misread its enemy.

A military industry emerges

Throughout 1941, America's willingness to continue diplomatic discussions with Japan was driven by the fact that it did not yet possess a military capable of fighting on both fronts. With isolationist tendencies still present, Roosevelt and other cabinet members could not divert full resources into expanding US forces – and some of its new equipment was being siphoned to Europe and China.

As early as 1935, the US Navy and government officials had decided against a move across the Pacific in response to potential Japanese aggression in the Philippines – something Yamamoto was convinced would happen and which drove him to develop the Pearl Harbor attack.

Had Japan taken its desired territory in South East Asia without striking against Hawaii, it is questionable whether the US would have been able to react, even if it wanted to. Such a move would not have sparked the same fervent national pride and anger among Americans who were joining the army in their thousands after December 7, and might not have been enough to allow Roosevelt to direct financial resource into his armed services. The move against Australia is a different matter, as the US had committed to defend shipping lanes to the country and this may have been a catalyst on its own.

These theories are just that, however,

and the point was rendered moot once the first bombs dropped on Oahu. A steady shift in opinion towards involvement in the Second World War became an unstoppable movement and the untapped American industrial might that Yamamoto so feared was about to be unleashed.

Within days of the attack there had been a remarkable culture change in the US unlike anything that had been seen before or since. War was no longer a distant threat, it was part and parcel of everyday life and people adapted their daily routines to aid scrap drives which collected vast amounts of aluminium and silk, among other useful materials. While economists have said the contribution compared to the overall resources needed was negligible, it further stoked patriotism among the population.

So too did round-the-clock salvage work which took place on the sunken vessels at Pearl Harbor. Led by Captain Homer N Wallin, ships which could be refloated were patched up and sent to shipyards in Pearl Harbor or on the mainland for more extensive repair – a total of 20,000 man-hours was spent underwater by divers working on the wrecks. While USS *Arizona*, USS *Oklahoma* and USS *Utah* were too heavily damaged, the remaining ships were all recovered and would see service in the Pacific War.

By early 1942, US aircraft, engine

and munitions plants were running 24 hours a day and the call soon went out for new workers. It was the final shot in the arm that America needed as it came full circle from the Wall Street Crash and it also aided in bringing more women and minority communities into the workplace. Before the conflict, women made up about 25% of American employees, but by 1945 that number had risen to 36%. During the same period, President Roosevelt had signed an executive order banning race discrimination in US defence plants and more than half-a-million African Americans migrated from the south to fill the jobs in the factories.

The whole country – all social sectors, big business, cities, rural communities – were unified in avenging Pearl Harbor but, despite the rapid military expansion which would ultimately prove to be an unstoppable force during the war and for remainder of the century, in the early part of the Pacific War Japan was still dominant.

At home, its citizens were buoyant as they celebrated the continued victories of the empire and greeted the aircrews of the Pearl Harbor strike forces as national heroes. Now on a war footing, America needed to demonstrate its strength, prove to Japan that it would not easily succumb and show its own citizens that it could and would hit back.

The Doolittle Raid

Long-term US goals were to protect its trading routes in the eastern Pacific, prevent precious resources reaching Japan and edge ever closer to its enemy by systematically retaking islands as it moved across the ocean.

A more immediate requirement, however, was a boost to American morale and before 1941 had ended, Roosevelt stated his desire for a bombing raid against the Japanese home islands as a show of force and as revenge for Pearl Harbor.

Admiral Ernest King – now Commander-in-Chief United States Fleet, the designation given to the new overall head of all three US Navy fleets – proposed that America strike the Japanese city of Tokyo and summoned his air operations officer Captain Donald B Duncan to discuss the possibilities.

There were no American bases in range for a bomber mission so the operation would have to launch from a carrier force, but no US bombers suitable for carrier use could deliver a payload powerful enough to cause the required damage. Duncan proposed a bold and daring plan which would see US Army Mitchell B-25 bombers lightened and launched from carrier flight decks.

Lieutenant Colonel James H Doolittle, a maverick USAAF pilot, was selected to lead the mission and despite not knowing any specifics his call for participants in a strike against the Japanese produced hundreds of willing volunteers.

To prepare the bombers for take-off on the carriers, Doolittle had catapults installed on shortened airstrips at Eglin Field, Florida, so pilots could simulate the proposed launch. Landing on the carriers would have been impossible so a hastily arranged plan was devised for the bombers

to head for friendly territory in China once their mission was complete.

At the start of April, 1942, just less than four months after the Pearl Harbor attack, the aircraft carrier USS *Hornet* steamed into the Pacific Ocean with 16 bombers aboard en route to a position between 400 and 650 miles off the coast of Japan.

It was at this time that the selected army pilots learned of the intended target and the news was met with delight. Navy airmen expressed their jealousy that they weren't part of the crews and reportedly offered up to as much as $150 to switch places with their army counterparts; none accepted.

As the fleet closed in on April 18 it was discovered by a Japanese patrol ship and although the destroyer USS *Nashville* quickly eliminated the enemy vessel there had been potentially just enough time for word to be sent back to land forces.

Despite being several hours and more

than 200 miles away from the intended launching point, the decision was taken to try and maintain the element of surprise and take flight immediately. The bombers were now set to arrive at their targets in daylight rather that during darkness and fuel – or the lack of it – became a potentially serious issue.

With just 467ft of runway in front of them, and with pilots who'd never launched from an aircraft carrier before, all 16 bombers managed to successfully get airborne and under way, flying in groups of two, three or four as they headed for 16 military and industrial targets in Tokyo, Yokohama, Yokosuka, Nagoya, Kobe and Osaka – although six schools and a hospital would be struck.

Some of the B-25s came under light anti-aircraft fire, and a handful of enemy fighters were encountered, but apart from that their run was relatively uneventful as they succeeded in their task of striking against the heart of the Japanese Empire. Making their approach at just a few hundred feet, the planes caused panic on the ground among civilians and was described by an Argentine diplomat who witnessed the force fly over his location as 'one of the greatest psychological tricks ever used'.

In material terms the damage was superficial at best, and paled into insignificance when compared to Pearl Harbor. It did, however, succeed in causing a loss of face among Japanese leaders, and the officer charged with defending Tokyo from air attacks committed ritual suicide in the aftermath because of his failure to prevent the bombings.

The makeshift planning of the Doolittle Raid meant that the Chinese airfields which were supposed to receive the bombers were never notified of the mission, although it wouldn't have mattered as the early launch prevented any of the pilots reaching their destinations due to lack of fuel.

Most crash-landed on the Chinese coast or on waters just off it and would owe their lives to the Chinese civilians who put themselves in danger to assist. Injured American pilots were transported

Lieutenant Colonel James H Doolittle, centre left, is pictured with fellow crewmembers in the days before the Doolittle Raid. ✪

It must have been an incredible sight to witness; land-based B-25s roars into the air off the deck of carrier USS *Hornet* en route to Japan. ✪

by whatever form of vehicle the locals could get their hands on and taken to the wartime Chinese capital of Chongqing. As a result, Japan launched the Zhejiang-Jiangxi Campaign in which it moved to ensure Chinese airfields could never be intended for American use again. As well as targeting this infrastructure, Japanese forces murdered at least 10,000 Chinese civilians during their search for pilots of the Doolittle Raid and anyone found in possession of American items was shot on sight. Some historians have since suggested that the death toll may have been more than 10 times this amount.

The B-25 crews who crashed in Japanese territory faced a similar fate and two were executed by firing squad after going on trial for bombing Japanese civilian targets. Another died while in confinement, but in the later war years the four remaining prisoners received slightly better treatment and survived long enough to be freed by American troops in August 1945, four years after their capture.

One bomber was landed successfully at an airfield in Vladivostok, Russia, but the aircraft was confiscated and the crew interned. The neutrality pact between Russia and Japan meant negotiations to return the pilots to the US were fruitless, but they were treated well and were eventually able to escape across the Russian-Iranian border to a British consulate. It was later revealed that Russia helped secure their release, but operated secretly to avoid angering the Japanese.

Doolittle was among the crewmembers who had reached China, but he was convinced that the loss of the aircraft would lead to his court martial once he returned to the United States. Instead, he was hailed as a hero and received the Medal of Honor and two-step promotion to brigadier general.

Japan's response was to take revenge for the embarrassment caused by American forces penetrating its air defences, and to establish how land-based bombers had managed to reach its home islands.

Yamamoto mistakenly concluded that the aircraft must have launched from Midway Island and so targeted a glorious final battle in the territory which would cripple America once and for all. What resulted was a pivotal turning point of the Second World War from which Japan would never recover.

Crewmembers of the Doolittle Raid stand outside the shelter where they hid following their crash-landing in China. ✪

CHAPTER 16

THE PACIFIC WAR

Japan awakens a sleeping giant

For six months after the Pearl Harbor attack, Japan appeared unstoppable as its forces extended out across the Pacific. The cracks would soon begin to show, however, and the untapped military might of America came to the fore...

As fighting spread across the Pacific, the Doolittle Raid – although causing negligible damage – decisively demonstrated that there would be no negotiated peace between Japan and America; and the US committed itself to achieving an unconditional surrender from Emperor Hirohito.

In response, Japan developed a 'defensive belt' strategy which would see it line-up a series of territories across the Pacific in order to form a barrier against any Allied offensives, and also cut off supply lines between the US and Australia. Believing that the Doolittle Raid had been launched from somewhere on Midway Island, Yamamoto also intended to invade the 2.4 square mile atoll and thereby prevent any chance of a repeated American strike

American troops in action on Luzon during the Pacific War. ✪

against the main Japanese homeland.

As a precursor, an operation was launched to take the key Australian strategic position of Port Moresby, New

Guinea, and the lightly defended Tulagi in the British Solomon Islands. Unlike the Pearl Harbor attack, the US was able to use intelligence gathering to uncover Japan's intentions and the invasion plan soon escalated into a major naval air battle in the Coral Sea.

The engagement was the first of many clashes in the Pacific ranging from small skirmishes to huge offensives involving tens of thousands of men on both sides. Ultimately, it was in the Coral Sea and at the subsequent Battle of Midway where the US established a firm foothold in the war. At that time, however, as America was striving just to keep pace, there were surely few who could have imagined the destructive way in which the conflict would eventually come to a conclusion in 1945.

The Battle of the Coral Sea

As Yamamoto put the finishing touches to his plan to lure America's naval aircraft carriers into a decisive showdown near the central Pacific island of Midway, he agreed that two of his fleet carriers, a light carrier, cruiser division and two destroyer divisions could be sent in support of Operation MO – the name designated to the operation to secure Port Moresby and establish an air base on Tulagi which would commence in May 1942.

The commander of the Imperial Japanese Navy's 4th Fleet, Vice Admiral Shigeyoshi Inoue, was given responsibility for the operation, and had requested the carriers from Yamamoto after damaging air attacks which Allied forces had mounted against Japanese army personnel in defending

New Guinea against an earlier offensive.

With the Japanese fleet advancing on the region, Allied codebreakers were able to determine the enemy's intentions and two of its aircraft carriers – including USS *Lexington* which had so crucially been absent from Pearl Harbor the previous December – along with supporting forces from Australia were sent to intercept.

On May 3-4, Japan successfully invaded Tulagi, but not without damage to several supporting warships inflicted by aircraft from American carrier USS *Yorktown*. Realising that US carriers were present in the area and the secrecy of their operation had not been maintained, Japanese carriers immediately steamed out into the ocean with the aim of finding and destroying any

Japanese light carrier Shoho *comes under attack during the Battle of the Coral Sea.* ✪

Allied forces they might encounter.

During two days of intensive air strikes the Japanese lost light carrier *Shoho*, but were able to cripple a US destroyer and fatally damage the aircraft carrier *Lexington* – the ships lost indicating that Japan had won a tactical victory.

However, the US was able to inflict heavy aircraft losses on both Japanese carriers, *Shokaku* and *Zuikaku*, while also physically damaging the former. The loss of air cover meant Inoue was forced to call off the proposed Port Moresby invasion, deciding instead to reconvene at a later date.

As each side retreated to count their losses, the four-day Battle of the Coral Sea became the first naval engagement in which the main ships had not fired on or even sighted each other – relying instead on their aerial arsenals. It was also the first time the Allies were able to prevent Japan from carrying out an intended invasion since the outbreak of the conflict. But, most crucially, it meant two of Japan's premier fleet carriers were out of action and unable to take part in Yamamoto's assault at Midway which was to take place the following month.

The Battle of Midway

The attack on Pearl Harbor had failed in its main objective: forcing America into retreat in order to stop the Pacific War before it had even begun. Japan had spectacularly misjudged its opposition and instead of breaking American morale it had only served to unify a segmented US against a common enemy.

However inexplicably, Japan – and Yamamoto – still believed that an aggressive act against capital ships would be enough to force America to capitulate and the leader of the combined fleet decided to lure American forces into a trap, end their influence in the region and capture Midway Island in the centre of the Pacific, adding it to the defensive perimeter his country was attempting to create. Midway could then be used as a launching point for attacks on the US west coast.

With Midway's proximity to Pearl Harbor, Yamamoto was sure that a surprise offensive there would draw the Pacific Fleet – now under the command of Admiral Chester W Nimitz – out into the open sea where the US aircraft carriers could finally be attacked and destroyed.

Even if the plan had been a resounding success it seems highly unlikely that it would have forced an American defeat, but as it was – and unknown to Yamamoto – while he was confirming the final stages of his operation the intelligence services which had been so crucial in uncovering the planned assault against New Guinea and Tulagi were busy relaying exact details of the plan to US naval officers in Hawaii.

On the morning of June 4, US combat forces took over where the intelligence efforts had left off and scouting planes soon discovered the location of the Japanese

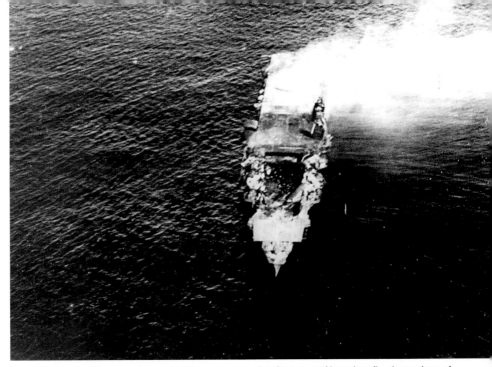

Japanese carrier *Hiryu* – photographed by a crew member from one of her aircraft – shows signs of damage as smoke rises from her deck. ✪

fleet, including carriers *Akagi*, *Kaga*, *Soryu* and *Hiryu* which had all launched aircraft against Pearl Harbor just six months before.

Douglas TBD Devastator torpedo bombers were dispatched almost immediately and the Japanese fleet – realising that this time it was not going to enjoy the element of surprise – was thrown into confusion. The chaos was compounded by the fact that Yamamoto had ordered hundreds of maintenance workers aboard the ships to continue repair work to aircraft which had been damaged during the Coral Sea engagement.

Admiral Nagumo who was in charge of the force at sea, just as he had been at Pearl Harbor, was able to scramble defensive Zero fighters against the bombers and 36 of the

42 Devastators were shot down with none inflicting significant damage.

Despite this initial failure of the US assault, the Zeros were now scattered and, as the action continued overhead, the fleet's carriers had drifted out of position leaving them isolated and vulnerable.

As ground crew on the ships attempted to refuel and rearm planes in preparation for a counter-attack, four squadrons of Douglas SBD Dauntless dive-bombers arrived and commenced a devastating attack.

Over the course of the battle, the US sank all four fleet carriers of the task force. They went down with all of their 322 aircraft and 5000 sailors on board. The Americans also destroyed a Japanese heavy cruiser, while themselves suffering from the loss of the USS *Yorktown* along with 147 aircraft and more than 300 seamen.

The Japanese attack on Pearl Harbor – while causing massive damage and huge loss of life – simply had not hit hard enough at the heart of the Pacific Fleet and a little more than six months later Yamamoto was made to regret this fact as his forces suffered a comprehensive defeat.

It may not have been appreciated at the time, but the US had now managed to do what Japan had not, as the loss of the four aircraft carriers proved to be a turning point in the Pacific War. With its limited resources already stretched, Japan now lacked the necessary power to defend its defensive belt in the Pacific – a fact which would become evident in the subsequent years. More important though was the loss of thousands of trained and experienced pilots, mechanics and engineers.

It would take time for the true impact of these appalling casualties to be felt, but their deaths meant a loss of manpower which might otherwise have allowed Japan to match America's sheer industrial might with ingenuity and skilled work. Without them, the smaller nation lacked the capacity to truly compete.

Japanese cruiser *Mikuma* burns below as Dauntless dive-bombers of USS *Hornet* stalk the skies above. ✪

A P-38 Lockheed Lightning – the type of aircraft chosen for the mission to assassinate Yamamoto. This particular example is a USAAF P-38G ⊙

The wreck of Yamamoto's transport plane, found a day after it was shot down over Bougainville. ⊙

Operation Vengeance

Japanese momentum had been halted by the events in the Coral Sea and the defeat at Midway which left Yamamoto – the brilliant strategist behind the Pearl Harbor attack – suddenly open to criticism. Determined not to follow traditional Japanese defensive doctrine, he proposed a continuation of his aggressive policies by speeding up the development of Guadalcanal airfield.

Part of the Solomon Islands, the Japanese had begun construction of a base there having invaded during its South East Asian expansion. Control of the territory, and the stationing of aircraft on it, was an extension of Japan's supposedly impregnable defensive belt and gave them a staging point from which to strangle US trade lines to Australia.

Realising the threat and buoyed by its first major successes of the conflict, the US launched a counter-offensive and in August 1942 American Marines led a band of Allied forces to overwhelm the Japanese soldiers tasked with defence of the new base, promptly capturing it.

A battle of attrition followed which saw several smaller skirmishes, but equated to considerable losses of men and equipment for both sides. America, now a fully operational war machine, could swiftly replace both personnel and machinery on the front lines while Japanese strength was beginning to diminish. Yamamoto committed extensive forces to his efforts, but he was unable to draw the entire Pacific Fleet into any kind of major action, instead just suffering steady losses to his already weakened force.

Despite occasional encouraging results, by February 1943 Guadalcanal had been fully lost and all attempts to reclaim it quelled. The once revered Yamamoto had lost the confidence of the Naval General Staff and could no longer convince them – as he had done about the Pearl Harbor attack – that aggression in the Pacific was the correct course of action. Left no other option than to comply with the traditional defensive position, Yamamoto decided to embark on a morale-boosting tour of the South Pacific territories which were still held by Japan, but he would not return to the home islands alive.

Once Roosevelt had learned the exact details of the intended trip through US codebreakers, he gave the command to Navy Secretary Frank Knox: "Get Yamamoto." The targeting of an individual political or armed services figurehead was unprecedented, but Roosevelt was aware of Yamamoto's status among Japanese military and civilians alike and the chance to avenge Pearl Harbor in such a direct and personal way – and so in-keeping with the narrative he had created – was an opportunity which could not be turned down.

The mission – given the designation Operation Vengeance – made its way through the various chains of command before Admiral Nimitz gave the go-ahead for a squadron of Lockheed P-38 Lightning aircraft to intercept Yamamoto's travelling party which would be in-flight from the Solomon Islands on the morning of April 18. Discovering their targets, the Lightnings engaged the two Mitsubishi G4M bombers – being used as transports – over the jungles of Bougainville, New Guinea, as well as the six Zero fighters escorting them. The first of the transports – which turned out to be the one Yamamoto was aboard – was hit with gunfire and as smoke poured from its left engine it crashed into the dense jungle below.

Japanese search planes flew overhead looking for survivors, and it would take a rescue group until the following day to find the wreckage, where they discovered Yamamoto's body. The death of a beloved navy leader in a militarist nation created a profound wave of sadness and dealt a hefty psychological blow. Such was the reverence felt for Yamamoto that he was given a full state funeral and was posthumously given the title of Marshal, awarded the Japanese Order of the Chrysanthemum and honoured by Nazi Germany also.

In the US – once the news finally emerged – it gave a great boost to military and public morale and, along with the growing success of operations in the Pacific, it laid the foundations for America to push further across the ocean and inflict final defeat on the Japanese Empire.

Yamamoto's ashes are carried from the battleship *Musashi* as they are returned to the Japanese home islands. ⊙

The now iconic image of US troops raising the Star Spangled Banner atop Mount Suribachi on Iwo Jima. The hard-fought battle for the island had cost the lives of more than 5000 American servicemen and 20,000 Japanese troops. ✪

The beginning of the end

Yamamoto's assassination and the Japanese defeat at Guadalcanal demonstrated the extent to which the course of the Pacific War had shifted, and the Allies followed it with a series of victories as forces pushed relentlessly through the Solomon Islands.

The stark reality of just how far Japan had overextended by failing to secure quick victory was becoming ever more apparent to government figures as its military continued to commit soldiers and services to the front lines.

A US marine comforts a fellow soldier who has just witnessed the death of his friend on Okinawa; a stark reflection of the death and destruction taking place in the Pacific. ✪

Making matters worse, Japan was also being crippled by unrelenting US submarine warfare which was targeting merchant vessels in the Pacific and preventing them from delivering vital supplies.

During 1943, as the tide turned, American factories were producing 7000 aircraft per month compared to 1500 from the Japanese; 500 American destroyers and destroyer escorts had been launched since 1941 compared to just 30 for Japan; and even though Japan held the advantage in terms of carrier production it simply did not possess the aircraft or trained crew to make them a viable threat.

As the American island-hopping campaign progressed, by the second half of 1944 US forces were closing in on the Philippines which it had surrendered two years prior. On October 20, US servicemen began landing on Leyte Island to spark the epic Battle of Leyte. The Japanese Imperial Navy, indignant and incensed that America could have managed to muster such manpower despite the resource-sapping Pacific conflict, focused its entire arsenal on defending the territory but after just five days it had all been repelled. Among the casualties was the veteran carrier *Zuikaku* – part of the Pearl Harbor strike group.

History would suggest that Midway was the point at which the tables turned, but America's successful invasion of Leyte was when the US firmly stamped its authority on the Pacific Theatre – it was at this time that

Japan turned to desperate kamikaze attacks and began to mobilise its considerable civilian population ready for battle.

With the Philippines secure the US was able to sever further supply routes to Japan – particularly with regards rubber and oil – and was now in a position to launch bombing raids against the home islands from air bases dotted across the ocean.

Attempting to secure further staging points for air attacks and neutralise Japanese defences, US forces embarked on campaigns to wrestle control of Iwo Jima and Okinawa which were among the most devastating and bloody engagements of the conflict; 5000 Americans were killed on Iwo Jima and 12,500 on Okinawa. Those losses were comparatively light when compared to 20,000 and more than 110,000 Japanese killed respectively on the two islands.

The staggering casualties demonstrated the way in which the war had become about unconditional victory at all costs – something which would never have been accepted by Americans in the era of isolationism before the Pearl Harbor attack. Military leaders, political officials, even the president, were willing to put thousands of American soldiers and seaman at risk to destroy Japan and were making preparations to land troops on the home islands. Before that, however, a secret government project was nearing completion – the success of which would render the invasion plan irrelevant.

America becomes a superpower

On April 12, shortly after being elected to an unprecedented fourth term as president, Roosevelt succumbed to a major stroke and for a short time after his death there were fears that the war effort would lose its way without the guidance of its driving force. It soon became clear that war policies and culture was too entrenched, however, and it was business as usual for the Allies as they sought to inflict a final and decisive blow against a weakening Japanese Empire.

The fire bombing of Japanese cities – carried out by fleets of Boeing B-29 bombers – was killing thousands of civilians across the country and decades of military rule was being questioned by an ever-growing peace movement. A 100-million strong civilian force was being prepared to resist against the inevitable invasion, but the equally inevitable massacre that would occur drew more and more dissenting voices. Of even greater concern was the idea that America could continue its bombing campaign for months or even years, wiping out the Japanese population before ever needing to set foot on the nation's islands.

Little did they know that the fire bombing was simply a prelude to something

B-29 bombers pass by Mount Fuji during a bombing raid against the Japanese home islands in 1945. ◎

far more devastating. On the morning of August 6 a three-year Allied project to create atomic weapons was realised as a B-29, named Enola Gay by its pilot,

dropped its payload on the industrial city of Hiroshima. The resulting blast killed more than 60,000 people on the ground within minutes; a far more devastating

Tokyo is photographed in ruins following a succession of US bombing campaigns against it. ◎

MEANWHILE IN EUROPE...

Four days after the Pearl Harbor attack – and with Japan and America having exchanged declarations of war – Germany and Italy backed their Axis partners by also making conflict with the US official.

After more than two years of finding ways around Congressional law to supply Britain and the Soviet Union with provisions and arms, Roosevelt could now tackle Germany and Italy head-on in Europe.

American troops first saw battle against their new enemies in North Africa as the Allies looked to push German and Italian forces into a retreat back across the Mediterranean Sea. Many Allied soldiers were killed in the offensive, but ultimately the operation proved successful in

regaining control of North Africa. The Allies then shifted their gaze to Europe.

Italy soon fell, although German soldiers would continue to resist in the country until the end of the war, and by 1944 attention had turned to France. The Soviet Union pressured Britain and the US to attack Germany from the west to relieve the strain on his forces in the east and, after several months of careful planning, Allied troops invaded at Normandy.

The D-Day landings were the largest amphibious operation in history, and by the end of the initial launch on June 6, more than 100,000 American, British and Canadian troops held beaches on the coast of France. A brutal, bloody and lengthy campaign ensued as the

Allies moved rapidly across France, often meeting stubborn German resistance and deadly counter-attacks. As part of the push across the country, Paris was liberated on August 19.

It would take nearly a year – and the deaths of hundreds of thousands of US and other Allied servicemen – but by the late spring of 1945 Germany appeared beaten. On May 2, Berlin surrendered to the Soviets and it emerged that Hitler – the man who'd held an iron grip on Germany for more than a decade – had committed suicide with enemy forces closing in.

By May 8 the war in Europe was officially over, and in the US full attention turned to eliminating the final Axis power left standing.

effect than any single bomb had ever been able to produce before. The subsequent spread of radiation had dire consequences for thousands more who survived the initial blast, shockwave and fires.

New American leader President Harry S Truman demanded a Japanese surrender, warning them to 'expect a rain of ruin from the air, the like of which has never been seen on this earth'. His calls were ignored.

Just three days later, the major seaport of Nagasaki was obliterated by the deployment of a second atomic bomb – the last to ever be used in warfare – with casualties once again in the tens of thousands. As Japanese high command reeled at the realisation America could produce and deliver these destructive weapons at will, the Soviet Union began an offensive against its forces in Manchuria. With far greater resources and more advanced equipment to call upon, the Russian troops inflicted severe losses on the Japanese in China – and knowing that America could blast Japan's entire civilisation from the face of the earth without ever having to land troops on the mainland there were only two options left: certain death or unconditional surrender.

On August 15, 1945, Emperor Hirohito announced that he was choosing the latter, but so deep was the Japanese conviction that defeat was not acceptable many officers staged armed mutinies or committed suicide. It would take until September 2, 1945, before the official Instrument of Surrender would be signed on the deck of the USS *Missouri* in Tokyo harbour, but individual militarists would resist for days, months and even decades on some of the more remote Pacific islands.

As was the case at the end of the First World War, America now found itself at an impasse: retreat into isolationism or be the leader of the post-war world. It emphatically chose the second, and has spent a large majority of the 75 years since exerting its considerable influence across all four corners of the globe.

A mushroom cloud over Hiroshima, the result of the US deploying the first atomic weapon ever to be used in conflict. ✪

A doctor from Nagasaki inspects the damage caused by the atomic bomb. Just a few days after this photo was taken, the doctor would die as a result of radiation poisoning. ✪

Japanese representatives stand aboard USS *Missouri* prior to signing the Instrument of Surrender. ✪

CHAPTER 17

JAPANESE INTERNMENT

America shows its dark side

Among the glorious tales of American victory in the Second World War, there were several chapters which the country would try hard to forget. One of them was its incarceration of many thousands of Japanese-American citizens accused of being potential sympathisers...

By 1945, despite the booming wartime economy, many American citizens still lived in poverty. Discrimination and institutional racism were still prevalent also, and despite its democratic and inclusive narrative America was fractured by division.

As euphoric celebrations welcomed US victory and a wave of patriotism swept the nation after the Pacific War, the fate of more than 100,000 Japanese-Americans who had been left destitute by a systematic and government-backed programme to exclude them from US society was widely ignored.

Under the pressure of conflict, the mass hysteria which surrounded the war effort had escalated into their forced internment in the months following the Pearl Harbor attack – removed on the basis they posed a potential security threat to the US military campaign.

People were taken from homes, farms, schools, jobs and businesses and sent to detention centres where many of them would be held for more than two years.

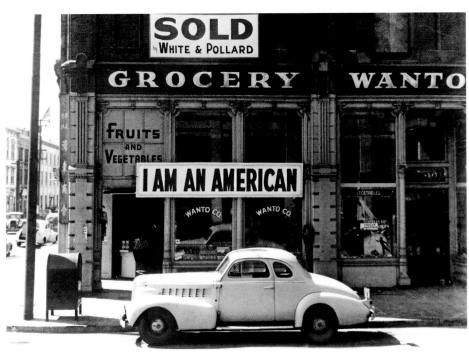

A Japanese-American shop owner put up this banner the day after the Pearl Harbor attack. It was photographed in March, 1942, just prior to his internment. ✪

Fears of a 'fifth column'

The wrecked Zero fighter of Japanese pilot Shigenori Nishikaichi. ✪

During the Pearl Harbor attack, Japanese pilot Shigenori Nishikaichi crashed his Zero fighter on the Hawaiian island of Niihau and was apprehended by residents – although they were initially unaware of the events unfolding just a few miles away on Oahu.

As news filtered across the territory, natives confiscated items from Nishikaichi who promptly sought assistance from three locals of Japanese descent. The trio obliged, helping the navy airman overcome his captors, find weapons and take hostages.

Nishikaichi was eventually killed, but as the details of the incident emerged many began to suggest the potential for secret pro-Japanese group in the US to emerge, and sabotage the war effort from within.

As the fear of espionage from a Japanese fifth column permeated from Hawaii to the US west coast, President Roosevelt

A Japanese family await the transport which will take them to their designated relocation centre. ✪

The harsh desert conditions are evidenced by a dust storm which sweeps across the Manzanar War Relocation Centre. ✪

signed executive order 9006 which called for the immediate exclusion of all Japanese-Americans from areas of military interest. It was left up to local authorities to put the exclusion into practice.

Given the concentration of naval forces on the west coast, officers and politicians determined that the entire region was of significant military importance and all Japanese-Americans living in the area faced the prospect of relocation.

By mid-1942 California and Oregon were home to 12 hastily erected camps which began housing internees. Conditions were poor. There was a lack of food, basic supplies and medicine; temperatures in the desert locations varied from 100 degrees-plus in the summer to sub-zero in the winter months; while housing was cramped, poorly lit and not private. Peoples' education and careers were put on hold – some were never

to be restarted – and interned citizens were forced to give up all their worldly possessions; many being business owners who'd come to the US in pursuit of the American Dream themselves, or had taken over from previous generations who had arrived in search of a better life.

At the same time, many young Japanese-American men were fighting for the US in the Pacific, and Japanese-Americans in Hawaii became vital to the domestic efforts in the territory making up a third of its total population. It was an incredible contradiction of freedom and oppression.

Lawsuits against the mass incarceration were filed, but the courts were among the institutional systems to be tangled up in wartime policies and America's top judges backed the relocation and the clear denial of civil liberties. On December 17, 1944, more than three years after the Pearl Harbor

attack, Roosevelt would announce the end of Japanese-American internment, allowing those who had been relocated to return home. As would be expected, attempts to integrate back into society were difficult and prejudice was still rife.

The affair cast a shadow over America, and it would not be the last instance of discrimination as throughout the next 25 years – and some would argue much longer – civil rights became the dominant domestic issue faced by the US.

These divisions demonstrated just how deeply American society had been affected by the Pearl Harbor attack. The dramatic reaction wasn't just an instinctive retaliatory move, it was the result of a seismic shift in the American character – and it was now a country prepared to go to whatever lengths it deemed necessary to emerge victorious.

Recognition of injustice

It would take until the 1980s before a full investigation into internment was launched, and it eventually concluded that the detention of Japanese-American citizens was not driven by military conditions but by discrimination, war hysteria and political failings.

At the end of the decade, President Ronald Reagan signed the Civil Liberties Act of 1988 which awarded $20,000 to each surviving detainee – the total reparations amounting to $1.2 billion.

On the 50th anniversary of the Pearl Harbor attack in 1991, President George H W Bush issued a direct executive apology by stating: "In remembering, it is important to come to grips with the past. No nation can fully understand itself or find its place in the world

President Ronald Reagan signs the Civil Liberties Act of 1988 which granted reparations for interned Japanese-Americans. ✪

if it does not look with clear eyes at all the glories and disgraces of its past. We in the United States acknowledge such an injustice

in our history. The internment of Americans of Japanese ancestry was a great injustice, and it will never be repeated."

CHAPTER 18

AMERICA IN THE MODERN WORLD

The legacy of Pearl Harbor

Beacon of liberty, warmonger, international activist, world policeman – to the modern world, these are just some of the ways American is seen and to many this is what it has always been. It's only since the Pearl Harbor attack, however, that the US has taken on these traits...

Pearl Harbor has fundamentally changed the United States of America. In the first half of the 20th century there had been the potential for the country to replace the British Empire as the dominating global force, but it took the Japanese strike, on its soil at the heart of its prized navy, to stir it from its slumber.

Yamamoto's worst fears had been realised as advances in industry and technology progressed rapidly, the US soon becoming the financial envy of the world. What Yamamoto could have perhaps never expected, however, was the wrath America would unleash following his failed efforts to enforce a favourable negotiated settlement – and the ruthless way it would prosecute its military campaign against Japan.

America has never done anything half-heartedly; from independence to Civil War to Manifest Destiny. When a narrative takes hold in the country it is all-consuming – and so it was after the Pearl Harbor attack.

What was it about December 7 that elicited such raw emotion and changed the character of a nation almost overnight? It is impossible to single out any one aspect of the attack. Whether it was the surprise nature of the assault, the death toll, the fact it occurred in an American territory – or a combination of these and many more factors besides – the resulting combination of fear, anger, resolve, patriotism and pride was immensely potent and fostered an insatiable desire to win at all costs.

And those costs were high indeed. The US lost more than 400,000 military personnel in the Second World War and a further 12,000 civilians were killed as a result of military operations. Isolationism had been founded on the idea that such loss of American life was unacceptable – particularly when it resulted from entanglement in European or other international affairs – but that argument had turned full circle with US troops now

willing to risk giving the last full measure of devotion to secure their country's victory.

More emphatic was the destruction America was willing to inflict on its enemies. Estimates suggest that anywhere between two and two-and-a-half million Japanese servicemen died in the fighting, with more than half-a-million civilians also paying the ultimate price. Many of the latter were killed as a result of devastating US fire bombing campaigns, and the launch of the first atomic weapons – America justifying the onslaught with the fact Japanese wartime industry had spread throughout the major cities and included civilians, who were also being mobilised as a defence force against possible invasion.

This approach to foreign policy – pursued under a banner of bringing freedom and liberty to all nations – would not end with the end of hostilities in the Second World War and would be something America continued for more than 25 years.

The Cold War

From left to right, Soviet leader Josef Stalin, American President Harry S Truman and British Prime Minister Winston Churchill are pictured in July 1945 at the Potsdam Conference. It was during this summit, as east and west put forward opposing arguments as to the direction of the world once hostilities were over, that the rising tensions between the two spheres would begin.
Courtesy, PA

As the US sought to dictate the course of the post-war world, it did continue one of its long-held beliefs – access to all commercial opportunities. Capitalism took a firm grasp of America, and large sections of society became more affluent than they ever could have imagined possible.

Many American political figures believed that isolationism and protective trade agreements after the First World War had played a significant role in the crippling economic depression which swept across Europe and had allowed the rise of brutal dictators in Germany, Italy and Spain.

Determined not to make the same mistakes – and needing a new unifying focus now Japan had been defeated – America's new might was directed at spreading its values and ideals. This course immediately put it at odds with the Soviet Union which maintained its belief in autocratic government and Communism as

a way of ensuring that it would never again face threats from the west as it had done from Nazi Germany.

As the Soviets used their military power to install communist governments in a series of eastern European nations, America called for self-determination for all of these countries including free and fair democratic elections. The rhetoric was ramped up as the 'capitalism versus communism' argument which was to shape global foreign policy for the next half-century commenced. In 1946, at a speech in Missouri, former British Prime Minister Winston Churchill declared that 'an iron curtain' had descended across Europe; warning that the continent faced the threat of a direct split between US allies to the west and Russian influenced nations to the east.

While only a political battle of wills at this point, the Cold War had begun in earnest and the two combatants used the newly formed United Nations organisation as the venue for their continuing arguments over their differing visions of how the post-war world would be shaped.

Rising tensions would soon take on a military dimension – not least because the Soviets enjoyed success within their own nuclear programme. In response the US, and the capitalist nations which were behind it, formed the North Atlantic Treaty Organisation (NATO) – a military agreement which, among other things, compelled participants to come to the aid of fellow members should they be attacked.

America's involvement was a bold statement that the era of isolationism was well and truly over, and it became the first official peacetime alliance the US had ever formed with a European power.

Aware that each possessed the ability to launch nuclear weapons, a stand-off ensued and both the US and Soviet Union dug in even deeper behind their chosen ideologies. The impasse allowed time for America to unfurl another of the great assets it had developed in the wake of the Pearl Harbor attack – an unrelenting propaganda machine.

It was a simple yet effective narrative: America and capitalism good, Soviet Union and communism bad. The US citizens who were enjoying a significantly increased standard of living in the 'golden era' of American capitalism soon bought into the story and were willing to defend their way of life by whatever means necessary.

There were, however, vast swathes of society which had been left behind and for whom the 'golden era' had been a time of economic struggle and cultural upheaval. While American and Soviet forces would never engage directly, as the Cold War intensified several proxy wars against communist regimes ensued.

Initially buoyant, Americans who were being sent thousands of miles from home to face likely injury and possible death would soon rebel against their country's relentless pursuit of global ideological dominance.

Vietnam

A combat journalist stands next to a fresh grave marked with an American flag during operations in Vietnam. Scenes such as this – and the terrible realities they captured – slowly turned US public opinion against the war. *Courtesy, PA*

By the early 1960s, America had already committed troops to stop the spread of communism from the Soviet- and Chinese-backed North Korea to South Korea, which was supported by the US. The result was a division of the countries in 1954 which still has major ramifications today.

At the same time, both America and the Soviets were rapidly increasing their nuclear arsenals in a frightening arms race which gave rise to the idea of 'mutually assured destruction' – if one nation launched against the other the resulting wave of missile strikes would completely wipe out both sides.

Attempting to move missile systems ever closer to each other, Soviet efforts to install weapons in Cuba – some 90 miles from the southern tip of Florida – sparked an international diplomatic crisis which is widely regarded as the closest any nation has come to launching an atomic or nuclear weapon against an enemy since the strike on Nagasaki.

The growing threat forced America to re-examine its position and prompted President John F Kennedy to counter the threat of communism in South East Asia by supporting the South Vietnamese government. The country was coming under threat from the communist North, with significant backing from the Soviet Union and China.

It wasn't until after the assassination of JFK that American combat troops were first sent to the country, but with Kennedy's successor – President Lyndon B Johnson – making it clear that South Vietnam would be protected from communism 'whatever the cost or whatever the challenge', it would not take long for thousands of soldiers to be sent to fight in the nation's jungles – many of them being drafted.

Perhaps a Soviet nuclear strike or act of aggression against America on American soil would have produced the same fervent reaction in the US as Pearl Harbor had, but without such an event people simply couldn't grasp what they were fighting for in South East Asia.

The bloody and costly conflict in Vietnam turned American politics sour and heavily damaged its previously booming economy. At home, too, the resentment was being driven by a rebellious counter-culture which was rallying against perceived injustices to minority communities who were now being forced to pay the price for a country which failed to afford them even basic freedoms.

A prolonged and deadly jungle war would suck the life out of American enthusiasm for foreign engagement and intervention, and the chaos would ultimately cost Johnson the presidency when he decided not to run in the 1969 election.

President Richard Nixon took office and inherited the conflict, and his administration immediately tried to improve Soviet-American relations and opened diplomatic negotiations with communist China. In military terms, however, the aggression America showed in the Pacific War showed no signs of slowing down as it launched ferocious bombing raids against the Vietnamese and employed new weapons such as napalm in a bid to burn the communists into submission.

Neither avenue was able to bring an end to the fighting however, and in 1973 American forces left South Vietnam under the guise of a peace agreement which left the country open and vulnerable to communist advances.

Nixon would continue to negotiate with the Chinese and Soviet governments, but the countries continued to subvert each other's ambitions throughout the world despite the outward desire for friendlier relations.

There would be a decade of détente, marred only by occasional diplomatic wrangling such as the American boycott of the 1980 Moscow Olympics in protest at the Soviet invasion of Afghanistan.

That incident rekindled the flames of the great battle of the mega-powers, and in 1979 Americans voted overwhelmingly to elect a leader who promised a much tougher approach to communism.

Ronald Reagan dramatically increased defence and military spending in the early 1980s, pressuring the Soviets with harsh language such as his memorable 'evil empire' reference. As Reagan upped the ante, it became apparent that all was not well within the Soviet Union itself as years of pouring money into foreign campaigns had left the nation's economy in tatters.

Despite a resumption of serious negotiations and the reforms of Soviet premier Mikhail Gorbachev, the rigid communist system finally collapsed. The Berlin Wall – constructed in 1961 as a literal and symbolic division between east and west – fell in 1989 to signal the end of Soviet domination in Europe and across the world, as well as the cessation of the Cold War.

The fall of the Berlin Wall signalled an end of division in Europe between capitalism and communism which had been drawn at the end of the Second World War. *Courtesy, PA*

With rescue efforts continuing in the rubble of the World Trade Center, George W Bush stands with firefighter Bob Beckwith and gives a rousing speech to workers from atop a burned out fire truck. *Courtesy, PA*

The 21st century

Victory – if that's how it is to be defined – in the Cold War maintained America's dominant geopolitical position, but it had certainly come at a price and the unifying desire to take on all comers and spread democracy across the globe had been replaced by a much more pragmatic and less aggressive approach.

It certainly wasn't a move back to isolationism, but that all-consuming national feeling to enforce and influence its ideology was no longer evident. Never was this more apparent than in the late 1990s when – as the fall of the Soviet Union led to internal struggles in the former Soviet states – it was a NATO campaign, albeit with the US as a central component, which responded to the Kosovan war.

Within two years of the new millennium, however, an event would occur on American soil which would bear a striking resemblance to the Pearl Harbor offensive and would lead to many similar outcomes.

The September 11 terrorist attacks in New York, Washington, DC and rural Pennsylvania became the defining moment for a generation of Americans who would and will never forget where they were when they first witnessed the harrowing scenes of two passenger airliners smashing into the World Trade Center towers and eventually bringing them down.

Like Pearl Harbor it was a surprise attack, it was an assault by a foreign aggressor and it killed thousands of American citizens. Despite being nearly 60 years since the events of December 7, the US reaction was remarkably similar: a sudden and overwhelming outpouring of patriotism and national unity, a definitive march to war and far-reaching political campaign which often stretched the moral boundaries and at times blatantly trampled over them.

It wasn't just the emotions which mirrored 1941; President George W Bush's impromptu address at Ground Zero on a bullhorn and the much later operation which killed the attack's mastermind Osama bin Laden bear remarkable resemblance to the Infamy Speech and the assassination of Yamamoto respectively.

September 11 hasn't, yet, had the same social impact as Pearl Harbor – America perhaps now too set in its ways for that to have occurred. But in the longer term, the growing threat of terrorism and the way America has ideologically lined up against it does seem to have some of the same hallmarks as the Cold War.

American author Mark Twain is often credited with the quote 'history doesn't repeat itself but it often rhymes'. We don't know what the future holds. In 50 years we could be looking back at the September 11 atrocities as a precursor to a much larger global conflict. Or perhaps it will be an isolated event, but one which will resonate through the ages. For America, Pearl Harbor has been both.

Either way, the echoes of history are certainly present and have rippled throughout the last 15 years. How far they will continue to resonate in the future remains to be seen.